HOW
TO BIKE
BETTER

HOW TO BIKE BETTER

Daniel Honig

Foreword by Michael Fraysse,
Manager and Coach, U.S. Olympic
Cycling Team 1984

Illustrations by Jack Eckstein

Produced by The Miller Press, Inc.

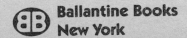

Ballantine Books
New York

The instructions and advice in this book are in no way intended as a substitute for medical counseling. We advise anyone to consult with a doctor before beginning this or any regimen of exercise. The author and the publisher disclaim any liability or loss, personal or otherwise, resulting from the procedures in this book.

Library of Congress Catalog Card Number: 84-91634

ISBN: 0-345-31846-3

Manufacturerd in the United States of America

First Edition: April, 1985

To the memory of my father, Jacob Honig

Acknowledgments

I would like to thank the following people for their help in making this book possible: Adam Honig, Angela Miller, Laurie Lico, Judith Cohen, Michael Fraysse, and Marilyn Abraham.

Contents

CONTENTS

Foreword

In my 25 years of experience as both a national team athlete and Olympic team manager and coach, I had not seen a book with all the basics of good cycling written in easy-to-understand terms until I read *How to Bike Better.* Only too often sports publications are comprised of page after page of complex information that even an expert cannot comprehend, let alone the average cyclist. These types of books get so technical and scientific that they miss the entire point.

This book *is* the point—and Dan has done it with a fresh, new approach to better biking. Because it is written in simple, everyday terms, it is a good source of reference for the advanced cyclist as well as the novice. The workouts described can be followed by the most proficient cyclists merely by increasing the intensity and distances.

How to Bike Better is ideal for cyclists of all ages and abilities. Dan has explained his training intensity in percentages rather than specific numbers so cyclists at all fitness levels can understand and use the workouts within their ability.

Biking is one of the most popular participation sports throughout the world, and a book such as *How to Bike Better* has been long overdue.

I conduct cycling clinics throughout the United States and around the world, and I will recommend this book to all the people with whom I come in contact.

—Michael Fraysse
Manager and Coach
U. S. Olympic Cycling Team 1984

Introduction

Biking is a relatively new sport. Modern-style bicycles became popular in the 1890s, and by 1895 the American cycling craze was reaching its peak. In those early days, recreation and transportation were the driving force behind cycling's tremendous popularity, but it wasn't long before some hearty individuals discovered the thrill of racing, on "stripped down" versions of the bicycle. That excitement is one of the reasons why cycling continues to be a favorite leisure-time activity.

Training methods and techniques have been developed, improved, and perfected since those first races. In the early 1980s the advent of the triathlon revitalized interest in bicycle road racing. The triathlon is a competitive athletic event combining swimming, cycling, and running in succession. From 1980 to 1984, close to one million runners, swimmers, and other athletes from noncycling backgrounds became active bicycle racers through participation in the triathlon. They were compelled to become proficient cyclists in the shortest time possible. Accordingly, training methods that produce fast results while remaining practical and easily understood were developed for the new breed of competitive cyclist.

Learning to bike better will be a milestone in your athletic career. I received my first bicycle on my seventh birthday, and marked my own first milestone the day I took off the training wheels. My second milestone came thousands of miles and 25 years later, when I purchased my first racing bike and began to train myself and others for competition.

As a coach for triathletes of all levels, I developed the training approach presented in this book. It is condensed from the rich history of bicycle racing techniques combined with the latest findings in exercise physiology and triathlon cross-training techniques.

Biking offers a great number of benefits even if you never compete in a race. These include cardiovascular fitness, enjoyment and relaxation, a feeling of oneness with nature, and the joy of competing against yourself as your form, speed, endurance, and self-confidence improve. This book will enable you to obtain the maximum benefits of cycling in the minimum amount of time.

So hop on your bike (if you already have one), strap yourself to the pedals (read the instructions on page 15 if you're not sure how), and let's go for a spin! Today is the ideal day to embark on the first ride of your new cycling career. Read this book tomorrow, when the forecast is for rain.

WHAT BIKING BETTER WILL DO FOR YOU

America is on the roll! With 72 million riders, cycling ranks as our second most popular sport. It's a fun way to exercise, a healthy release for tension, and it gives us an outlet for competitive impulses that are too often repressed by modern living. It puts us outdoors and keeps us on the move.

If you are interested in a physical-fitness program that takes you beyond the realm of your immediate surroundings and introduces you to a new form of pleasure and mental relaxation, this book will guide you to your goal in an easy-to-follow, concise method. From selecting a bicycle, dressing for the ride, and learning fundamental skills, this program will get you out of the bike shop and onto the scenic roads in the shortest time possible. Then you will learn how to use your bicycle as a *tool* to improve your overall fitness.

If you already bike, better biking technique will help you derive the greatest benefits, pleasure, and success from long-distance touring or road-racing competition. Both novice and advanced rider will learn how to structure a cycling program that suits your own schedule—and make cycling an integral part of your lifestyle.

Biking is the most economical means of transportation, and the bicycle is the most efficient means of transforming human power into speed and distance. You will learn how to utilize the full potential of the bicycle by employing proper cycling form.

Biking allows people to travel and explore the country in a unique way. The ability to ride 100 miles in a single day gives us a new understanding of the land and challenges our perceptions of speed and distance. The bike is a pollution-free vehicle, easy to maintain, and parking spaces are readily available anywhere. A feeling of oneness with nature, the exhilaration of speed on a long downhill, and the thrill of exploring new places are within our realm when we are cycling.

Biking is a "gentle" sport. The bicycle supports the entire body weight so we can exercise without the risk of injury to the joints, ligaments, and tendons that is associated with running. It is a common misconception that cycling demands less of the cardiovascular system than running. However, an hour of cycling actually provides the same stimulation and benefits as a running work-out of the same level of intensity.

If you are a runner, cycling is a valuable way to stay fit while recovering from an injury that necessitates abstinence from running. Biking allows you to discover your psychological and physical limits without a weak Achilles tendon or fallen arch to hold you back. Alternating cycling and running workouts will refresh you mentally and break the boredom associated with pounding out mega-miles. Many world runners include rigorous cycling workouts in their training routine.

An old saying reminds us that there can be no happiness in the absence of health. For many Americans, staying healthy means being physically fit. According to Dr. Kenneth A. Cooper, author of the acclaimed book *Aerobics,* cycling, running, and swimming are the top three aerobic sports. Aerobic exercise improves cardiovascular fitness through a sustained elevated heart rate. Endurance increases as our heart, circulatory system, and muscle strength improve. After several weeks of biking you will find that longer and faster rides become easier as you reach new levels of fitness and health.

The American College of Sports Medicine

(ACSM) recommends cycling to improve overall cardiovascular endurance. Cycling fulfills the ACSM's three basic requirements because 1) it uses the large muscle groups, 2) it can be sustained for long durations, and 3) the smooth circular pedaling action is rhythmical and does not put undue stress on the body.

Biking keeps the upper legs, waist, and hips trim, and is an excellent way to lose weight. After roughly two hours of riding, the body uses up energy reserves and begins to metabolize fat for energy. A prolonged exercise program trains the muscles to rely more heavily on fat reserves. As you incorporate the following eating and exercise methods into your weekly routine, you will find that proper nutrition, reduced calorie intake, and a wise cycling program keeps your body slim and fit!

Whether you bike for fitness, enjoyment, or competition, this book will lead you to your goals by improving your riding skills. Emphasis is placed on technique, since cycling performance peaks when the bike and body function as a unified piece of machinery.

The fitness lifestyle that better biking provides can only be obtained by adapting the 3-P principle: practice, perseverance, and patience. Practice your techniques, persevere in your training, and have patience as you ride toward your long-term goals.

② ELEMENTS OF BIKING BETTER

SELECTING AND FITTING YOUR BICYCLE

A quality touring or road-racing bicycle is lighter in weight and more responsive than an ordinary sport bike. Sized and fitted correctly, a good bicycle will put you on the road to better cycling.

Good bicycle shops stock a variety of American- and foreign-made bicycles, and should offer you personal attention and assistance.

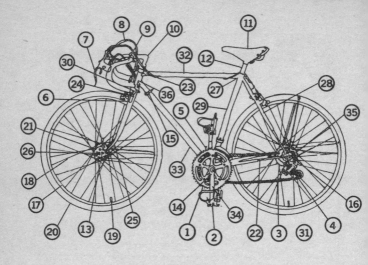

Figure 1   Key to Bicycle Parts

1. Chainwheel
2. Pedal
3. Chain
4. Rear derailleur
5. Front derailleur
6. Caliper brake
7. Brake lever
8. Brake cable
9. Handlebars
10. Handlebar stem
11. Seat (saddle)
12. Seat post
13. Quick-release skewer
    (for instant wheel removal)
14. Bottom bracket
15. Gear-shift levers, front
    and rear
16. Freewheel gear cluster
17. Rim
18. Spoke
19. Valve
20. Tire
21. Hub (high-flange type)
22. Chainstay
23. Lug
24. Fork crown
25. Fork
26. Front wheel dropout
27. Seat cluster lug
28. Seat stay
29. Seat tube
30. Head tube
31. Tension roller, rear derailleur
32. Top tube
33. Downtube
34. Cotterless crank
35. Rear wheel dropout
36. Headset (top and bottom)

Bicycle selection is made according to frame size. The saddle, handlebars, and toe clips are then adjusted to fit your body. By making educated decisions and following proper procedures, you will have a bicycle that is completely coordinated for maximum energy efficiency and better cycling.

FRAME SIZE

A properly sized frame ensures comfort and balance, and facilitates maximum cycling efficiency.

Standard frames range from 19 inches to 27 inches. This measurement is the distance from the center of the crank to the top of the seat tube.

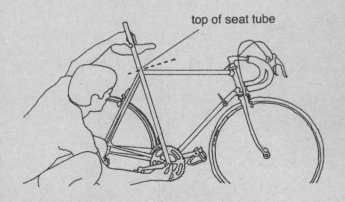

top of seat tube

Figure 2

Frame size is determined by body height. If the frame is the wrong height, then the pedals, handlebars, and seat will not fit your body proportions. Your posture will suffer, and biking efficiency will be greatly reduced.

The most common, but incorrect, way to determine frame size is to stand over the bike and choose a frame that is approximately one inch shorter than the crotch. This method is based on the safety requirements for dismounting the bike, but does not relate to cycling efficiency.

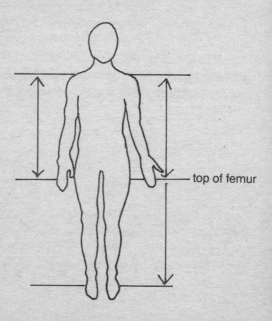

top of femur

Figure 3

To correctly determine your frame size, stand barefoot and measure the distance from the top of your upper thigh bone (the femur) to the floor. Subtract 13.5 inches (34 cm.) from this number to obtain a good estimate of your frame size. Always choose the closest smaller-size frame. For example, if you measure 37 inches from the floor to the top of the femur, $37 - 13.5 = 23.5$, then you would select a 23-inch frame.

Buy the right size frame and then adjust the bike to your body. The following guidelines for positioning and adjustment are useful for initial set-up. As your biking technique improves, you should experiment with slight alterations. Make changes one at a time, in small increments, allowing at least 100 miles of riding before new adjustments are made. Naturally, the final criterion is comfort.

SADDLE ADJUSTMENT

Proper saddle adjustment gives you optimum pedaling efficiency, balance, and handling. The saddle is raised or lowered, moved forward or backward, and tilted to fit your specific needs. This requires three independent measurements and adjustments, and a few simple tools.

Height: Put on your cycling shoes, sit on the saddle, and bend forward to hold the top of the handlebars. Place one heel flatly on a

Figure 4   Measuring Saddle Height

pedal that is in its lowest position. When the saddle height is correct, your knee is bent slightly while full heel-pedal contact is maintained. Repeat this measuring procedure for both legs.

Test the height by pedaling backward while keeping both heels flat on the pedals. Your knees should still maintain a slight angle when the pedals reach their lowest extension. If you must slide from side to side to maintain heel contact, then your saddle is too high. If your knee bends more than a few degrees when the pedal is at its lowest position, then the saddle is too low.

Fore/Aft: To determine correct fore/aft position you will need a small weight suspended on a string (a "plumbline"). Sit squarely in the saddle and grasp the handlebars above the brake levers. Insert your shoes into the toe clips as far as they will go and bring both pedal cranks to a position horizontal to the floor.

Suspend the plumbline from the bony protuberance just below the outside of the knee. Fore/aft position is correct when the weight falls through the axis of the front pedal.

Figure 5   Determining Saddle Fore/Aft Position

Tilt: To measure saddle tilt, simply lay a yard-stick or broomhandle across the saddle and note the angle it makes with the top tube.

The front of the saddle should tilt very slightly upward. If you find this uncomfortable, start with the saddle parallel to the top-tube and increase the angle after roughly 100 miles of cycling.

Under no circumstances should the seat tilt downward. This will cause you to lean

Figure 6   Measuring Saddle Tilt

too far forward onto the handlebars, leading to sore or numb palms and fatigue in the hands, arms, and shoulders.

Bicycles are designed to support 45 percent of the rider's weight on the front wheel and 55 percent on the back wheel. If additional weight is put on the handlebar and front wheel, rolling efficiency and steering ability will suffer.

HANDLEBAR/STEM ADJUSTMENT

The handlebar drops should be parallel to the ground or angled slightly upward in the direction of motion.

Figure 7   Handlebar and Stem Adjustment

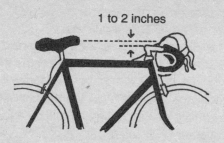

Figure 7a

The stem is the L-shaped piece connecting the handlebars to the frame. As a rule of thumb, the top of the stem should be one to two inches below the top of the saddle.

To adjust handlebar height to your body, sit on the bike with your hands on the handlebar drops and your elbows slightly bent. In this position the handlebars should be in a straight line of vision with the front wheel hub, thus blocking it from view. If you can see the wheel in front of the handlebars then you are probably too cramped (and upright) for efficient cycling.

Try raising and lowering the handlebars until the correct position is achieved. The length of the stem extension may have to be changed if you are to obtain this position and still be within the one to two inches prescribed. Stem extensions are usually available in 10-mm. increments from 60 to 140 mm. (2.5 to 5.5 inches).

TOE CLIPS, CLEATS, AND STRAPS

Toe clips and straps are necessary for both racing and touring. Used properly, they increase cycling efficiency by approximately 30 percent.

When mounted correctly, clips, cleats, and straps become one unit with the pedal. Wasted foot movement is minimized and power delivered to the pedals is maximized. The system allows you to apply energy throughout the entire pedal revolution—pulling as your pedal comes up and around from the back.

When the foot is fully inserted into a properly adjusted toe clip, the ball of the foot will be directly over the pedal axis. In this position there should be some clearance (1/8 inch) between the front of the shoe and the toe clips. This clearance prevents friction or pressure on the toes during long rides, and allows the cleat to engage and disengage the pedal easily. The strap holds the shoe onto the pedal.

Cleats are used predominantly for racing. The cleat is rigidly attached to the wooden bottom of the cycling shoe with nails or screws, beneath the ball of the foot. The pedal is then inserted into the pedal grip on the cleat. Mounting the cleat so that the toes are pointed slightly inward (pigeon-toed) increases cycling efficiency and reduces risk of knee injury.

CAUTION—improperly aligned cleats are a major cause of cycling-related injuries.

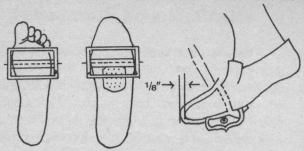

Figure 8   Proper Foot Positioning

Being strapped to the bicycle can be an
intimidating experience for the novice cyclist.
Getting in and out of the toe clips with cleated
shoes will take some practice and maybe one or
two embarrassing falls. The awkward period will
pay off later by improving power transmission
from legs to pedals, aiding in the development of
proper circular pedaling technique, increasing
hill-climbing capabilities, and reducing foot fatigue on long rides.

BIKING ATTIRE

Biking attire is designed for safety, comfort,
and efficiency. A helmet is the most important
safety item. For comfort you will want to investi-
gate various jerseys, shorts, socks, gloves, and
cold-weather riding gear. Efficiency is maximized
with quality cycling shoes.

HELMETS

You must wear a good hard-shell helmet whenever you are on the road. It can save your life. Leather or other soft-shell helmets simply do not offer the same life insurance as a hard-shell helmet constructed of high-impact polystyrene.

Head injuries account for over 80 percent of all bicycle-related deaths. They are usually the result of a fall, accompanied by a sharp blow to the head. When the head is unprotected, the brain may be smashed against the interior of the skull, causing loss of consciousness, coma, or even death.

Superior impact protection is the most important helmet feature. The outer and inner liners must be able to absorb the shock of a severe blow. Hard-shell helmets offer impact protection that is far superior to that of even the best soft-shell helmets.

The helmet shell must also prevent sharp objects from penetrating or abrading the skull. The more surface area of the head and scalp that is protected, the better the helmet. Open and therefore vulnerable areas for ventilation and/or weight reduction should not affect the structural integrity of the shell.

At the same time, a good cycling helmet must offer adequate ventilation. Forty percent of our body heat is lost through the head. During hot-weather riding, it is essential to provide sufficient ventilation so perspiration is evaporated and heat build-up under the helmet is reduced. Ventilation holes are also ideal for squirting water on the scalp during long, hot rides. The holes may be taped over during cold-weather riding.

Other important helmet features are a solid retention system, light weight, bright color, and unobstructed visibility. The retention system, usually composed of a strap and buckle, is by far the most important. The best-designed helmet will be rendered useless if it is not securely attached to the head during a fall. Always try to rip off the helmet before a ride, to be sure that it will not be torn loose during a fall. Heavy helmets may lead to neck soreness. The helmet should cover as much of the head, neck, and scalp as possible without obstructing vision. Bright color is important since the helmet is the highest point on the rider and should stand out to motorists.

Biking accidents are inevitable and safety precautions are of the utmost importance. The necessity of a good hard-shell helmet—to protect against impact, penetration, and abrasion injuries—cannot be overstressed.

SHOES

Good-quality cycling shoes with mounted cleats are necessary for best results in cycling competition.

Most cycling shoes are currently made in

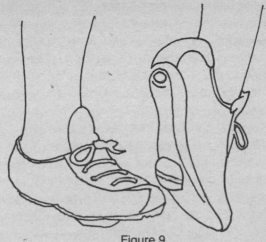

Figure 9

Europe. Widths and lengths vary from country to country: Italian-made shoes are known to be quite narrow, while shoes produced in Belgium are quite wide. Before purchasing the cycling shoe, try on several brands to see which offer the firmest, most comfortable fit. The shoe must limit foot movement but not cramp the toes. With a snug fit, minimum motion is lost through the foot-shoe-pedal link. A well-constructed shoe prevents the foot from sliding around or rolling inward toward the arch. It also prevents blistering.

A rigid sole plate, traditionally made of wood, prevents the shoe from "wrapping around" the pedal during the downstroke. The hard sole also prevents pedals from digging into your feet and numbing them during long rides.

The upper should be made of soft, supple leather with plenty of holes for ventilation. These holes also allow water to drain from the shoe on rainy days. The leather upper tends to stretch with continued use. If the shoe becomes too stretched out, resilient foam inserts can be used to take up the slack.

Cycling shoes are not made for walking. The rigid soles, with an elevated heel and an angle under the ball of the foot, enhance cycling technique but make walking quite uncomfortable. Shoes designed for walking and riding are appropriately called "touring" shoes, and have a semi-rigid rubber-sole bottom. The touring shoe usually has several ridges molded into the rubber sole, which act as cleats. Although touring shoes compromise biking efficiency, they serve their purpose quite well and should be considered by all touring cyclists.

SHORTS

Cycling shorts have a padded liner sewn into the crotch, usually made of chamois material. Chamois provides cushioning and reduces friction and chafing.

Wool and cotton are traditional materials for cycling shorts. Synthetic fiber and wool or cotton blends greatly enhance durability. Modern-day racing shorts, called "skin shorts," are made of Lycra-Spandex materials. These lightweight shorts

cling snuggly to the body, allow complete free-
dom of movement, and wear extremely well.

Shorts should extend half-way down the
thigh to prevent them from riding up or bunching.
They should be seamless or have internal stitching
that does not cause irritation or unnecessary
rubbing. If you have crotch irritation or saddle
sores, apply a water-based lubricant such as
Noxzema to reduce friction and irritation in this
sensitive area.

The traditional black color is more than just
fashionable. Black material absorbs heat to warm
upper leg muscles, and does not show stains
from a well-oiled leather saddle.

Shorts should be washed frequently to
prevent build-up of infectious bacteria. If you
plan to become a serious biker it is wise to invest
in two pairs of shorts so you will always have a
clean, dry pair available.

JERSEYS

The cycling jersey is designed to keep you
warm, protect against surface skin abrasion during
a fall, provide rear pockets for carrying food or a
water bottle, and stand out to motorists. It should
be long enough to cover the small of the back
when you are in the maximum bent-over riding
position. Three back pockets, as opposed to two,
are essential for carrying a spare water bottle in

the center pocket, where it will not rotate to one side.

The jersey should fit snugly around the torso to minimize wind resistance. The material must be comfortable and smooth so it does not cause chafing, and should whisk perspiration away from the skin. Cotton, wool, and wool blends are ideal for cycling jerseys, as they are cool in summer and warm in winter. The neck and sleeves should be made of a soft-ribbed material with non-chafing seams, and the neck should be cut high to protect against the cold. The jersey should have a zipper to keep a snug fit and allow ventilation when needed.

GLOVES

Cycling gloves usually have half fingers, a mesh back, and an adjustable Velcro wrist strap. They have thick leather padding in the palm to absorb shock and to prevent numbness, blisters, or raw spots on the hands during long rides.

Since we instinctively extend our hands to break the impact of a fall, gloves also offer protection against scraping. Padded palms on the gloves are also helpful in dislodging pieces of glass or road debris that may become imbedded in the tires.

When taking off wet gloves after a long ride, it is best to peel them from the wrists, inside out, rather than trying to loosen each finger separately.

SOCKS

Socks are a matter of personal preference. Cyclists are seen wearing thin, thick, or no socks at all. Racers should be forewarned that the United States Cycling Federation (USCF) requires the use of socks in all sanctioned races.

The best socks are made of cotton, wool, or any blend that contains 50 percent or more of either material. They should be no more than ankle height, so they do not absorb too much water and become heavy during rainy-day rides. For women cyclists, tennis socks (peds)—with the pom-poms removed—are ideal biking socks.

Socks protect the feet against blisters or irritations that may be caused by rough inner stitching in the cycling shoe. Socks will also absorb perspiration that drips down the leg and may lead to blistering if allowed to drain into the shoe.

COLD-WEATHER OUTFITTING

When you are biking you are creating your own wind chill factor. Riding at a speed of 15 mph automatically creates an additional 15-mph wind chill effect. On a day with 10-mph winds and a temperature of 30° F, the combined wind chill factor of 25-mph will result in a frigid − 4° F on your body (see Wind Chill Factor chart, page 25). When cycling, your upper body, hands, and feet are particularly susceptible to cold and must be protected.

The lower the temperature the more layers you should wear. You can "peel" the layers off as the day gets warmer, or as your body warms up. Polypropylene material is an excellent bottom or "thermal" layer, as it whisks perspiration away from the skin. This is extremely important if you are stopping and starting often, because sweat can freeze on your skin.

A cotton turtleneck over the polypropylene will keep your neck warm, trap in heat, and absorb the sweat from the polypropylene. Over this wear a wool sweater or bike shirt—thickness depends upon the temperature. If it is unusually cold or windy, a wind-breaking layer of Gore-Tex or nylon is a valuable topping.

Layering the legs with wool over polypropylene or standard thermal bottoms is also a good idea for very cold days. Two thin layers of socks are better than one thick pair—polypropylene and wool is the ideal combination. Shoe covers are available to fit all shoe models. Cycling shoes with air holes are not recommended for cold weather.

Mittens are fine and may be worn on the hands as long as they do not hamper braking ability. A wool hat or nylon cycling cap may be worn under the helmet.

WIND CHILL FACTOR
Equivalent Temperature on Exposed Flesh

Air Temperature (°F)							
35°F	21	16	12	7	5	3	1
30	16	11	3	0	-2	-4	-4
25	9	1	-4	-7	-11	-13	-15
20	2	-6	-9	-15	-18	-20	-22
15	-2	-11	-17	-22	-26	-27	-29
10	-9	-15	-24	-29	-33	-35	-36
5	-15	-25	-32	-37	-41	-43	-45
0	-22	-33	-40	-45	-49	-52	-54
-5	-27	-40	-46	-52	-56	-60	-62
-10	-31	-45	-52	-58	-63	-67	-69
-15	-38	-51	-60	-67	-70	-72	-76
-20	-45	-60	-68	-75	-78	-83	-87
-25	-52	-65	-76	-83	-87	-90	-94
	10mph	15	20	25	30	35	40

Combined Wind Speed (mph)
(bike speed and wind speed)

PRE-RIDE CHECKLIST

Before each ride you should check, inspect, adjust, or tighten the following:

- *Brakes:* Check position on rim of front and rear (f/r) brake shoes. Tighten brake nuts if necessary. Check each brake separately by squeezing the brake liner as hard as possible, and trying to push the bike forward. It should not move. Clean grime from brake pads (and rim) with alcohol if necessary.

- *Tires/Rims:* Check condition of f/r tires. Check for correct air pressure. Spin each tire separately. Check for trueness (alignment) of rim. Shake rims to inspect cone/axle tightness. Correct or tighten as necessary.

- *Seat Post/Saddle:* Hit the nose of the seat down with the palm of your hand to check for tilt tightness. Hit nose of seat from side to side to check seat post tightness.

- *Handlebars/Stems:* Lean on the handlebar drops and try to rotate them downward. Tighten if the slightest movement is detected. Hold front wheel firmly between your legs and try to rotate handlebars from side to side. Tighten if necessary.

- *Pedals:* Check to see that the pedals are screwed all the way in. Twist from side to side and look for play (looseness between the pedal and the crank). Pedals should spin freely.

- *Chain:* Check tension in chains in highest and lowest gears.

- *Cables:* Check f/r brake and derailleur cables for fraying or kinks. Replace if required.

- *Quick-Release:* Check f/r quick-release mechanisms for tightness. They should be centered in the fork tips.

- *Drop Test:* Lift the bike and drop it on both wheels from a height of six inches. Listen for rattles or loose parts and tighten if necessary.

TOOLS FOR THE ROAD

The age-old saying "an once of prevention is worth a pound of cure" couldn't be truer than for biking. You should never go on a ride without taking enough tools and spares to get you back home safely, in case of a breakdown or mishap. The following are recommended as the minimum equipment for any ride.

Short Rides

- Spare sew-up tire (rim glue or tape)
- Patch kit—complete for clincher tubes
- Air pump
- Hard-shell helmet
- Tools—tire irons, pocket-knife screwdrivers, adjustable and Allen wrenches as required for bike

Long Rides

- All of the items for a short ride
- One spare rear brake cable (may be cut for front)
- One spare derailleur cable
- One additional sew-up tire (total of 2)
- One tube (clincher tires)
- Water bottle
- Money and personal items
- Cycling gloves
- Food
- First-aid kit—8 Band-Aids (1" wide), 1 roll adhesive tape (3/4" wide), 1 gauze bandage

roll (2" × 5 yards), 2 gauze bandages (3"
× 3"), 4 adhesive pads (2" × 3"), 1 tube
first-aid antiseptic cream, 1 bottle iodine/
Mercurochrome, 4 antiseptic towlettes, 8
aspirins, 1 penknife or scissors

- Rag and hand cleaner (or disposable thin
surgical gloves)

- Cyclocomputer (recommended)

Hot-Weather Rides

- All of the above for short and long rides

- Sunglasses

- Extra water bottle (total of 2)

- Sunscreen (primarily for neck and shoulders)

Cold-Weather Rides

- All of the above for short and long rides

- Leg and arm warmers

- Thin ski cap (under helmet)

- Winter cycling gloves or mittens

- Windbreaker and/or long-sleeve thermal
jersey

- Shoe covers to keep feet warm and/or dry

Night Rides

- All of the above for short and long rides
- Front and rear lights (check battery fresh-ness)
- Reflective tape on helmet
- Reflective vest

3 BIKING FORM

CYCLING FUNDAMENTALS

Riding with style and efficiency requires correct body position, proper pedaling technique, precise gear shifting, and smooth braking. You must understand and master these fundamentals before you can begin training to improve distance, speed, and endurance.

The key to comfortable riding is keeping your body relaxed at all times. Tension wastes energy that you need toward the end of the ride. Always concentrate on relaxing your upper body, especially your grip on the handlebars.

BODY POSITION

Correct body position is essential to better biking. This refers to the torso posture and the position of the grip on the handlebars. It is virtually impossible to cycle for long periods without changing your body position.

There are three basic handlebar positions, requiring varying degrees of forward bend. Each has specific advantages. Regardless of your position on the handlebars, your elbows must always be bent to absorb road shock transmitted through the handlebars to your body.

Top Bar Position

This is the most comfortable and relaxed way of cycling, and should be used to relieve muscle tension in the upper back, neck, and shoulders.

The back is bent from the waist at a 45° angle. It is straight and not cramped. Unfortunately, the large frontal area presented by this position makes it very comfortable, but aerodynamically inefficient.

Figure 10   Top Bar Position

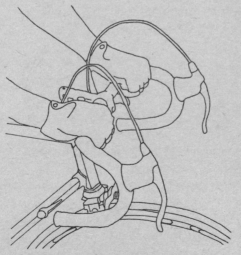

Figure 11   Top Bar Position (detailed)

33

Figure 12   Brake Lever Position

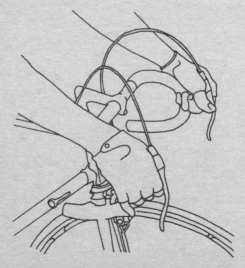

Figure 13   Brake Lever Position (detailed)

34

Brake Lever Position

This provides the best combination of comfort, minimum wind resistance (frontal area), and good visibility.

The body is at an angle of less than 45°, which eases back tension and sore hands. This is the posture most often used by road racers, because it offers maximum use of the buttocks muscle (gluteus maximus) without putting undue strain on the back. It is also a safe riding position, because the hands are capable of grabbing the brake levers without shifting position.

This is the preferred uphill cycling position,

Figure 14   Drop Position

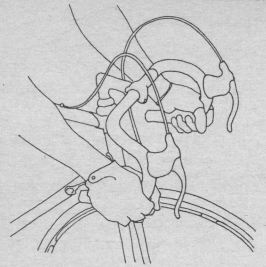

Figure 15   Drop Position (detailed)

and gives you increased leverage if you raise
yourself off the saddle (see Hill Climbing, page 67).

Drop Position

Although racers are most often depicted in
this position, they will never spend more than 30
percent of their total riding time in this position.

This is the preferred position for sprinting,
accelerating, or riding at speed in a head wind,
because it offers minimum wind resistance, easy
access to (and maximum leverage on) the brakes,
and maximum steering control. However, this is
the least comfortable riding position, and causes
shoulder and back pain if maintained for too long.

PEDALING

Pedaling technique has a marked effect on biking efficiency. Competitive cyclists, and some experienced touring cyclists, can be distinguished by their smooth-flowing pedaling motion. Novices often make the mistake of resting through part of the pedal revolution. Pedaling should be a continuous circular motion, with energy applied throughout the entire rotation.

The knees should move up and down in a fluid (not jerking) motion, with no side-to-side movement. They should be as close as possible to the top tube at the height of each stroke, to maximize muscle efficiency, reduce the risk of knee injury, and cut down on the wind resistance offered by the frontal profile.

There are four phases of each pedal revolution. Imagine the circular rotation of the pedal as the face of a clock. From one to five o'clock we press downward, transmitting the greatest amount of power in the stroke. At the end of the downstroke we begin the pull-backward phase, which lasts from five to seven o'clock. This is followed by the upward-pull phase, from seven to eleven o'clock. The forward phase, from eleven to one o'clock, completes the revolution.

Maximum power transmission occurs on the downstroke, but this accounts for only 30 percent of the total range of motion. The remaining 70 percent of motion transmits approximately one-

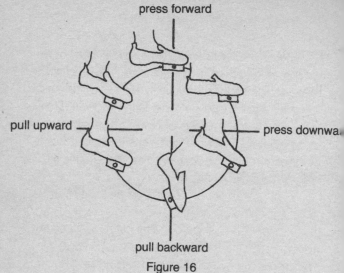

Figure 16

third of the power that can be delivered during one complete pedal revolution.

A common beginners' mistake is to focus only on the downstroke. You must concentrate on applying pressure to both pedals throughout the entire revolution. When one foot is in the downward phase, remember that the other leg should be pulling through the upward phase.

Maximum efficiency throughout the entire revolution can only be achieved if the rider is equipped with properly adjusted toe clips, cleats, and straps. All phases of pedaling require firm contact between the foot and the pedal.

Cadence refers to the rate at which the pedals turn. A cadence of 90 means that the pedals are turning at a rate of 90 revolutions per minute (rpm). To determine pedal cadence, count the number of times your right pedal reaches its highest point during a 10-second interval. Multiply this number by 6 to calculate rpm.

A good pedal cadence on level terrain is 80 to 100 rpm. This rapid cadence is known as "spinning," and is usually achieved when cycling in a low gear. It is the most efficient way to cycle during long races, because it retards lactic acid build-up. If you are unable to maintain a cadence of 80 to 100 rpm for extended periods, try switching to a lower gear, but do not lose pedal resistance. Spinning may feel unnatural at first, but it is crucial to better cycling.

Spinning will also bring out mistakes in your biking technique. If the gear you are pushing is too high, your upper body will tend to bounce off the seat. If you reduce gears and still find yourself bouncing, your saddle may be too high. Correct saddle height is necessary for efficient pedaling. Check saddle position and make adjustments as suggested on pages 9–13.

SHIFTING GEARS

Bicycle gears enable the rider to maintain steady cadence over varying terrain, wind conditions, and one's own level of fitness or fatigue. In low gears, turning the pedals becomes easier. In higher gears there is greater resistance, requiring increased pressure on the pedals. Mastering proper shifting technique takes hours of practice, but is essential to proper pedal cadence and better biking.

The novice should begin riding on a level road, in a comfortable gear, at a steady cadence of 80 to 90 rpm. Practice riding at or close to 80 rpm until you are able to judge and maintain this cadence naturally. After you master the feel for proper cadence, you are ready to start shifting.

When it becomes necessary to change gears, ease up on your pedal pressure but do not stop pedaling. Place one hand on the top (straight) part of the handlebars for maximum control while shifting the gear lever with your free hand. If you hear a slight rattling sound, move the gear lever until the rattle stops. Immediately resume normal cadence, look at the road ahead, and anticipate any conditions that will require further shifting. Shifting gears should be smooth and flowing. Never shift through more than one gear at a time.

Anticipation is the key to efficient gear shifting. When you encounter an incline, shift to a lower gear to maintain cadence. As you proceed up a hill, you will probably have to decrease your cadence. Always try to maintain a minimum cadence of 50 rpm (see Hill Climbing, page 67).

Inexperienced cyclists tend to ride in high gears, thus increasing the risk of knee injury and decreasing long distance cycling efficiency. The amount of time that you can "push" a gear that is too high is limited. Human physiology is such that we can go for longer distances if we maintain a relatively fast and easy cadence than if we pedal at a relatively slow and strenuous cadence.

A basic understanding of gearing technology is essential for advanced cyclists. The 12-speed bicycle has two front sprockets (chainwheels), and six rear sprockets (freewheels). Sprockets are measured by the number of teeth around their circumference. Racing bikes commonly have two front sprockets with 52 and 42 teeth, and six rear sprockets with 13, 15, 17, 19, 21, and 24 teeth.

Gear ratio is the relationship between the front and rear sprockets. Calculating gear ratio is useful so that you know which front/back sprocket combinations have similar ratios.

$$\text{Gear ratio} = \frac{\text{number of teeth on chainwheel}}{\text{number of teeth on freewheel}} \times \frac{\text{wheel diameter}}{\text{(in inches)}}$$

For example, if the chain is on the 42-tooth sprocket on the chainwheel and the 19-tooth sprocket on the freewheel, with a standard 27-inch wheel, the gear ratio would be $42/19 \times 27 = 59.7$. On the same bike, a $52/24$ combination would have a 58.5 gear ratio—very similar to the first combination, and resulting in similar pedal resistance.

A well-designed bicycle will have few similar gear ratios. The accompanying gear-selection

GEAR RATIO CHART
(27-inch wheel)

		Number of Teeth on Freewheel (Rear Sprocket)											
	13	14	15	16	17	18	19	20	21	22	23	24	25
40	83.1	77.1	72.0	67.5	63.5	60.0	56.8	54.0	51.4	49.1	47.0	45.0	43.2
41	85.2	79.1	73.8	69.2	65.1	61.5	58.3	55.3	52.7	50.3	48.1	46.1	44.3
42	87.2	81.0	75.6	70.9	66.7	63.0	59.7	56.7	54.0	51.5	49.3	47.3	45.4
43	89.3	82.9	77.4	72.6	68.3	64.5	61.1	58.0	55.3	52.8	50.5	48.4	46.4
44	91.4	84.9	79.2	74.3	69.9	66.0	62.5	59.4	56.6	54.0	51.7	49.5	47.5
45	93.5	86.8	81.0	75.9	71.5	67.5	63.9	60.8	57.9	55.2	52.8	50.6	48.6
46	95.5	88.7	82.8	77.6	73.1	69.0	65.4	62.1	59.1	56.5	54.0	51.8	49.7
47	97.6	90.6	84.6	79.3	74.6	70.5	66.8	63.4	60.4	57.7	55.2	52.9	50.8
48	99.7	92.6	86.4	81.0	76.2	72.0	68.2	64.8	61.7	58.9	56.3	54.0	51.8
49	101.8	94.5	88.2	82.7	77.8	73.5	69.6	66.1	63.0	60.1	57.5	55.1	52.9
50	103.8	96.4	90.0	84.4	79.4	75.0	71.1	67.5	64.3	61.4	58.7	56.3	54.0
51	105.9	98.4	91.8	86.1	81.0	76.5	72.5	68.8	65.6	62.6	59.9	57.4	55.1
52	108.0	100.3	93.6	87.8	82.6	78.0	73.9	70.2	66.9	63.8	61.0	58.5	56.2
53	110.1	102.2	95.4	89.4	84.2	79.5	75.3	71.5	68.1	65.0	62.2	59.6	57.2
54	112.2	104.1	97.2	91.1	85.8	81.0	76.7	72.9	69.4	66.3	63.4	60.8	58.3

Gears (in inches)

Number of Teeth on Chainwheel
(Front Sprocket)

chart gives gear ratios for other chainwheel and freewheel combinations.

Note that a 12-speed bicycle offers only 10 practical gear ratio combinations, because the two extreme sprocket positions—the largest chainwheel with the largest freewheel or the smallest chainwheel with the smallest freewheel—should be avoided. With these combinations, the chain will be at too great an angle to the teeth, resulting in increased friction in the drivechain mechanism, and premature wear of the sprocket teeth.

BRAKING

The key to proper braking is anticipation and smoothness. Correct braking procedures are easily explained in theory, but mastered only with many miles of practice and experience.

During braking, the weight of the rider and the bike is transferred forward onto the front wheel. In normal situations, approximately 80 percent of the braking action is done by the front brake. This is why you must always check the condition of the tire, brake pads, and their position on the tire rim before each ride.

It is best to use both brakes at all times. Some riders prefer to use the front brake most of the time, and resort to the back brake only during emergency stops. *Always use both brakes in emergency stops.* If you apply the front brake only, you risk being thrown forward over the handlebars or having the front wheel slide out of control.

Unfortunately, the most critical braking situations will occur with little warning. When braking abruptly, brace your arms (keeping elbows slightly bent), slide your weight back in the saddle, and stabilize your position by pushing your feet against the pedals.

The best braking position—and the one of maximum leverage—is the drop position (see page 36 for illustration). This position is commonly used in long, fast descents or when cornering at high speeds.

Many cyclists ride predominantly in the brake lever position (see page 34 for illustration), because the first two fingers of the hands are already in position to grip the brakes. Although this position does not provide maximum leverage on the brakes, it is good for gradual speed reduction before cornering, and for well-anticipated stops.

On long downhills, proper braking requires "feathering"—applying a light, on-and-off pressure to the brake levers. This technique prevents rims and brake pads from overheating.

Incorrect braking often leads to falls, especially during a turn or when road conditions are slippery from sand, loose gravel, or rain. You must allow longer braking time on wet or slippery surfaces. The initial contact between the brake pad and the rim will only wipe away surface water, and wet roads reduce tire adhesion. Brakes must be applied gently, as abrupt braking on slippery surfaces causes skidding and/or loss of control.

CAUTION—never apply the brakes once you've entered a turn.

TRAINING TECHNIQUES

To become a better cyclist in the fastest time possible, concentrate your efforts on building speed, endurance, and strength. This is best achieved with a routine that combines long slow distance (LSD), interval, high intensity training (HIT), and wind-load simulator workouts. It's recommended to monitor your progress and workout intensity with a cyclocomputer.

As your body adapts and becomes stronger in response to physical stress, your cardiovascular fitness and muscle strength will improve, and both your aerobic (endurance) and anaerobic (speed) abilities will increase.

In his pioneering book *Aerobics*, Dr. Kenneth Cooper states that cardiovascular fitness can be developed by regular, mildly stressful exercise that forces the heart, lungs, and circulatory system to work harder than usual. Aerobic exercise is done at a steady, leisurely pace, never exceeding the level at which oxygen can be adequately

supplied to the active muscles. Aerobic activity
can be sustained for extended periods of time.
Long slow distance training improves that time by
adapting the body to increasing work loads and
building cardiovascular endurance.

Anaerobic exercise is strenuous activity that
demands more oxygen than the lungs and blood
vessels are capable of supplying to the muscles.
As we cross the anaerobic threshold the body
enters a state of "oxygen debt." Anaerobic activity, such as strong bursts of speed, can be sustained for a relatively short time before a rest
period is needed to replenish the oxygen supply.
Lactic acid, a by-product of anaerobic exercise,
rapidly accumulates in the muscles, leading to
immediate soreness and rapid fatigue. Through
intervals and HIT rides, we can condition the body
to sustain longer periods of anaerobic exertion.

Long slow distance rides are "easy" workouts, while intervals and high intensity training are
"hard" workouts. A hard workout is one that is
done on the threshold of anaerobic metabolism,
at 85 percent of the maximum heart rate. An easy
workout is done at 70 percent of the maximum
heart rate.

To calculate maximum heart rate, simply
subtract your age from 220. Thus, the maximum
heart rate for a 30-year-old is $220 - 30 = 190$.
Using this example, a hard workout would be
done at a heart rate of 162, while an easy workout
would be done at 133.

Experts have found that to improve cardio vascular fitness, the body must engage in aerobic activity at 70 to 85 percent of the maximum heart rate for 30 minutes, at least 3 times a week. In most cases, maintaining a heart rate of less than 65 percent of the maximum is of little or no benefit to the cardiovascular system.

The most efficient way to build speed, endurance, and strength is to follow a workout program that balances the three training techniques—LSD, intervals, and HIT—and allows sufficient recovery time between hard workouts. Alternate hard and easy workouts and monitor your physical indicators for symptoms of overtraining.

LONG SLOW DISTANCE TRAINING (LSD)

Long slow distance training is the groundwork for any fitness program. It provides aerobic stress that develops a powerful heart while increasing blood circulation, lung capacity, and efficient aerobic metabolism within the muscles. Your body learns to utilize oxygen more efficiently, and becomes better adapted to metabolizing fat for energy in the late stages of a long ride.

LSD rides should be done at a steady cadence of 80 to 100 rpm while maintaining 70 to 80 percent of your maximum heart rate. Beginners should train in gears between 54 and 60 inches, while advanced cyclists and racers will usually do their LSD training in gears between 63 and 74 inches (see Gear Ratio chart, page 42).

The beginners' LSD workout should cover 10 to 20 miles, and experienced cyclists should ride for 30 to 50 miles. As cardiovascular fitness improves you will increase speed and endurance while exerting the same amount of effort. Your goal should be to increase your mileage by 5 to 10 percent per week. If you are training for a specific event, your LSD ride should eventually cover the entire race or touring distance.

INTERVALS (INT)

Interval training is one of the most important techniques in a racer's arsenal. It increases speed by developing and strengthening the muscle fibers that produce energy by anaerobic metabolism.

Interval workouts are done at a faster and harder pace than your desired race pace, maintaining a cadence of at least 90 rpm. A typical interval workout consists of one minute of fast riding, followed by a one-minute recovery period of slower pedaling. The fast interval should be performed at 85 to 95 percent of the maximum heart rate—well over the anaerobic threshold. Your heart rate should drop to 120 or below before you begin the second interval. This routine

should be repeated 10 times. Follow the 10 repetitions with an easy 10- to 15-minute cool-down
ride, which is necessary to flush lactic acid out of
the muscles. Advanced cyclists may then do
another group of 10 repetitions.

When training for longer races, an alternative
interval routine is recommended. This consists of
eight repetitions of two-minute fast intervals, each
followed by a two-minute rest period. In general,
as the length of the intervals increases, the number
of repetitions decreases. Increase the intensity of
interval workouts as your fitness improves, but do
not expect any marked differences in your performance in less than six weeks.

Interval training should not be started before
a rider has logged between 1,000 and 1,500 miles
of LSD training. Beginner cyclists should never do
more than one hard interval workout a week.
Racers will do two interval workouts per week,
allowing two to three days of recovery before
attempting another.

Interval training involves a process of breaking down and rebuilding muscle tissue, so there is
a greater risk of injury than in other forms of workouts. A 10- to 15-minute warm-up and cool-
down session before and after workouts helps
speed recovery of damaged tissues. These ses-
sions should include the stretching exercises as
illustrated on pages 102-110.

Most racers find interval training the most
difficult from a physical and mental point of view.

The need to constantly check the watch and perform on command makes this type of workout seem like drudgery, but it is the key to successful competitive cycling.

For variety, cyclists may try other forms of interval workouts. Fartlek training is an unstructured workout that originated in Scandinavia as a training method for distance runners. In Swedish, "fartlek" means "speed play." It involves incorporating random intervals of speed riding whenever you feel the desire to do so. Choose a landmark approximately one-quarter of a mile up the road and ride to it as fast as you can—as if you were in the final stretch of a race. Allow your heart rate to return to 120 before attempting another all-out effort. Whatever the length of the speed segment, the recovery period should be spent spinning in an easier gear, while maintaining sufficient resistance in the pedals.

It is easy to let oneself become "lazy" during fartlek, either doing too few intervals or not pushing hard enough for intense bursts of speed. It requires a lot of discipline but is always more enjoyable than straight intervals, and the physical benefits are as significant.

Common fartlek routines include racing toward a specific landmark, braking during the last quarter-mile up a long hill, or sprinting to catch another cyclist or slow-moving vehicle. One of the most enjoyable forms of fartlek is group riding, where each rider takes a turn leading the pack.

HIGH-INTENSITY TRAINING (HIT)

This third type of workout combines the endurance benefits of LSD with the speed benefits of intervals. It includes intense aerobic and moderate anaerobic exertion. Accordingly, the target training heart rate is 85 percent of the maximum heart rate—at the high end of LSD training and the low end of INT training.

HIT rides are shorter distances than LSD rides, but longer than interval workouts. They are most effective when done at close to your desired race pace. Modified speed intervals should be incorporated into HIT rides, with slow recovery in between.

The latest research shows that endurance can be improved in the shortest time through high-intensity training, because it stimulates the most rapid changes in muscle fibers, capillaries, and heart and lung capacities.

WIND-LOAD SIMULATORS (WLS)

This piece of equipment, invented in 1980, revolutionized the concept of cycle training. It is unique because it re-creates the effect of wind resistance on your pedaling—the faster you pedal, the more difficult the effort becomes, just as if you were moving. A wind-load simulator enables you to structure and carry out a fully controlled

workout indoors, anytime. This great advancement
in training methods has just begun to impress the
world of cycling with the dramatic improvements
that a well-designed program can provide.

This mechanical device is quite simple to use.
The front wheel of the bike is usually removed
and the front fork of the bike is clamped solidly in
place on the WLS. The bike is supported by the
WLS, and the rear wheel of the bike maintains full
contact with the fan wheel on the simulator.

The heart of the WLS is in the fan wheel,
which rotates at the same speed as the rear
wheel. The rolling resistance of the fan wheel
increases exponentially, to increase resistance as it
would be experienced by a moving bicycle.

The WLS makes it possible to cycle indoors
and achieve a "purer" training experience than if
you were pedaling down the road. Not only does
it allow you to ride during inclement weather, but
it eliminates interference from rough roads, moving vehicles, traffic signals, hills, corners, etc. The
controlled environment allows you to focus completely on your pedaling and shifting techniques,
and on your progress. If WLS workouts become
boring because there is no visual stimulation from
the great outdoors, you may find that television,
music, or conversation is convenient and makes
the time zip by as your legs are spinning at a
cadence of 90 rpm.

The wind-load simulator can be used for
LSD, interval, or HIT workouts. Thus, specific work-

Figure 17 Wind-Load Simulator

outs scheduled for a day when it is impractical to ride outdoors can be performed in an identical manner indoors, on your own bike, which has been fit and adjusted to your body.

The basic training principles apply to WLS workouts. For practical reasons, a workout on the WLS should last from 30 minutes to one hour. The following are typical examples of LSD, intervals, and HIT workouts performed on a WLS.

LSD Workout (aerobic training)

5–10 minutes: For the warm-up, select an easy gear that offers moderate resistance and spin at 85–100 rpm. Your heart rate should stabilize at 60–70 percent of its maximum.

10–60 minutes: Concentrate on spinning at 85–100 rpm and maintaining the heart rate at 70–80 percent of maximum. Novices should begin in a gear of 58–63 and advanced riders in gears of 65–74. If you are maintaining proper cadence and cannot elevate your heart rate to target level, then switch into a higher gear. Similarly, if your heart rate is above its aerobic threshold, then shift to one gear lower to ease your load.

5–10 minutes: For this cool-down period, a 60″ (42 × 19) gear is suggested.

Interval Workout (anaerobic training)

10–15 minutes: Warm-up in a 60"–63" gear
(42 × 18 or 19) for a mini-
mum of 10 minutes. Intervals
generally require a longer
warm-up period than LSD
training.

20–30 minutes: Repeat *either* of the following intervals 10 times:
- 60 seconds pedaling full
  speed (minimum 120 ca-
  dence), and 60 seconds
  recovery intervals (90
  cadence).
- 2 minutes pedaling full
  speed, and 3 minutes
  recovery interval.
- A progression of 30 seconds hard and 60 seconds
  easy, followed by 45 seconds hard and 60 seconds
  easy, adding 15 seconds
  on each repetition of the
  hard segment, to 90 seconds hard and 60 seconds
  easy, and then repeating
  the progression in reverse
  order. Cadence should
  never drop below 90 rpm,

while advanced cyclists will be spinning at 120 rpm or more. Recommended gears are 74–100 (52 × 19–14) for the full speed intervals and 67–76 (52 × 21 or 42 × 15) for the rest intervals.

10–15 minutes: Cool-down in the same gear as the warm-up.

Note: If you are unable to do 10 repetitions of the hard workout, make a note of how many complete sequences you performed properly and proceed to the cool-down phase. In your next interval training session, try to exceed the number of repetitions by one. Increase your gear by one as soon as the 10 repetitions become easy.

HIT Workout (aerobic/anaerobic training)

5–10 minutes: Warm-up in a comfortable gear, spinning at a cadence of 85–100 rpm in a 60"–64" gear.

30–45 minutes: This can be performed in one of the following ways:

- Pedal at 90–100 rpm, maintaining 85 percent of your maximum heart rate for 30 minutes. This should be done in a gear of 74–94 (52 × 19–15), depending on your fitness level.
- Do similar workouts as in anaerobic workouts but double the length of the recovery part of the interval between successive bursts of speed.

5–10 minutes: Cool-down is suggested in a 60" gear (42 × 19) or in the same gear used in the warm-up phase.

Note: The HIT workout is "heavily" aerobic and "moderately" anaerobic. Adjust the gears and monitor your heart rate—80–85 percent of your maximum heart rate is your goal for maximum benefit from HIT. The workouts will improve your cycling form and will increase your effectiveness in determining race pace.

CYCLOCOMPUTERS

These ingenious products are the latest high-tech training aid from the electronics industry. A cyclocomputer is light, compact, and easy to mount and remove from the bike. It will make your workouts more efficient by monitoring a wide range of bike/rider functions and providing accurate data. Correct use of cyclocomputers can aid in increasing your speed, improving your technique, conserving valuable energy, and can add enjoyment to your workouts with mental stimulation.

A well-designed unit has a digital display showing speed, cadence, elapsed time, distance, average and maximum speeds, and total mileage. It is mounted on the handlebars and is always visible. Cyclocomputers use a non-contact sensor to detect revolutions of the wheel and pedals. The signals are fed into a microprocessor in the main unit, where the input is processed and displayed. The basic unit costs between $35 and $65 and will operate for many months on a standard battery.

The most basic cyclocomputer function is speed. A constant readout of your speed helps you select the most efficient gear. By checking your speed, you will know if you should be sitting or standing off the saddle on a hill. Likewise, you will be able to determine whether pedaling is actually increasing your speed on a downhill run. You will discover the correct combination of gearing, cadence, and body position to make each ride most efficient.

Cadence monitoring is invaluable in perfecting winning spinning techniques, and is one of the most important functions of the cyclocomputer. Spinning is a basic cycling technique, and an accurate cadence readout will help you maintain your desired cadence. Cadence display is especially valuable in helping the novice cyclist determine correct spinning gear. Some of the more sophisticated cyclocomputers can be programmed to let the cyclist know when a pre-set minimum and maximum cadence is reached. Thus, if you determine that you should be pedaling between 80 and 100 rpm, the cyclocomputer will emit a beep tone when you go above or below the pre-set limits.

The elapsed-time function is actually a conveniently placed stopwatch, useful in determining how long it takes to ride a measured distance. This is very helpful during interval workouts, which consist of short, measured bursts of speed followed by longer recovery periods. The total elapsed time divided by the total distance will give you an indication of your average speed.

The distance function should be reset to zero at the start of each workout or ride. This will give you a sense of how many miles you can cover in a specific time and will build your confidence for taking "longer" rides that require a high state of mental preparedness.

Average speed can be calculated by elapsed time and distance traveled. But why bother to do the calculation when the cyclocomputer will do it for you? Your average speed is a good indication of cycling ability since it is the net result of your personal level of fitness and environmental factors such as wind, rain, hills, and adverse surface conditions.

The cyclocomputer is a very useful tool for improving the quality of your training, whether it be LSD, interval, or HIT workouts on the road or on a wind-load simulator. It allows you to "take charge" of your training and perform at your desired level.

ADVANCED SKILLS

The advanced cyclists should practice riding a straight line, cornering, drafting, and hill-climbing techniques, and incorporate them in their workouts. These advanced skills must be mastered if you want the competitive edge.

RIDING A STRAIGHT LINE

This is one of the most elementary skills a cyclist must master. Although it may seem simple, there are actually many cyclists who cannot ride a straight line. It requires many hours of practice to maintain correct and steady steering.

Practice riding a straight line by following a painted line along the side of the road during an LSD ride. Try to stay on the line or within four to six inches of its edge. Success depends upon proper body positioning and shifting. The upper body should be totally relaxed, with elbows bent and arms acting as shock absorbers. Steering should be done primarily by shifting your weight back so you have a light grip on the handlebars. The rougher the surface, the tighter your grip.

When shifting, have one hand in the top handlebar position for maximum control as you shift with the other hand. Avoid shifting during situations when you need both hands on the handlebars to maintain control.

Riding a straight line maximizes cycling safety and efficiency. Drivers know where you are going, and you also decrease the risk of being side-swiped when you stay in your own lane. In races or group riding, a straight line conserves energy and is a prerequisite to drafting.

DRAFTING

Also known as "riding a wheel," this is a common practice in long-distance touring or racing. Proper drafting can conserve up to 30 percent of your energy expenditure during a ride. It can be dangerous if executed improperly, but it increases your enjoyment and efficiency when done correctly.

While riding, most of our energy is spent displacing the air in front of the body. The faster we ride, the greater the wind resistance. Technically speaking, wind resistance increases with the square of speed. This means that if we double our speed from 10 mph to 20 mph, wind resistance increases by a factor of four. Thus you work four times as hard to double your speed. However, if

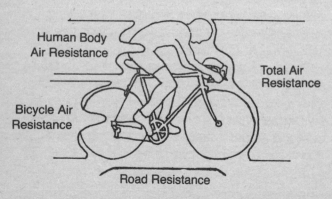

Figure 18

you ride closely behind someone, this effort is significantly decreased.

Drafting gives you the sensation that you are being pulled in another rider's wake, because the rider in front is braking the wind for you and reducing your wind resistance. Maximum benefit from drafting is realized when you are riding within one foot behind a rider. The effect is significantly increased at a distance of six inches.

The closer you can get to the rider in front, the better the drafting effect. However, extreme caution is advised against getting too close behind or alongside another rider. Any contact between your front wheel and the rear wheel of the other rider will most likely cause an accident.

Do not stare at the wheel in front of you— look at the road ahead. Pedal smoothly to maintain a safe wheel-to-wheel distance, and avoid braking if possible. Using the brakes will slow you down and create a gap that will require an extra burst of speed to bridge. Braking can also be very hazardous to a rider who is trying to draft off of you. When a gap is formed, accelerate smoothly and don't overshoot the wheel of the rider in front.

It takes long hours of training and quick reflexes to perfect your drafting skill to a point where you are able to ride your own line at proper cadence and maintain a relatively smooth pace that will allow you to maximize drafting benefits.

CORNERING

Biking at speed around a corner is a novice cyclist's nightmare. Correct cornering technique reduces your chances of skidding in the turn, and is vitally important to racing. Executed properly, cornering can be fun and exciting. Follow these four basic steps for proper cornering:

1. *Preparation:* Determine the speed at which you want to negotiate the turn. This decision is based on road surface conditions (dry, wet, oily, sandy, or gravelly), sharpness of the turn, its banking, and your cornering skill.

   You will often want to decrease your speed for a turn. Braking, if necessary, *must* be done before entering the turn. *Never* apply the brakes once you have initiated the turn, since it will probably result in a fall.

2. *Choose a path:* The path should be a smooth arc throughout the turn. Wide arcs are recommended because they allow you to maintain more of your speed as you recover from the turn. Tight arcs require speed reduction, which wastes energy upon acceleration.

   Enter the turn from as far to the outside as safely possible, following an arc that crests at the tightest section of the turn.

   Let your eyes follow your line about 15 feet ahead of the bike. It is critical that the line be

maintained throughout the turn. Once commit-
ted to a turn, any changes in direction, speed,
or body position can be disastrous. In a turn it
is possible to change direction at slow speeds,
but at high speeds a change in handlebar
direction will usually cause you to lose control.

3. *Body position:* The laws of motion dictate that
the bike and rider lean into the turn. Centrifugal
force will be pulling you upright, and you must
pull against it when you lean into the turn.

The degree of the lean depends upon the
path, speed, road conditions, and the banking
of the curve. Higher speed, well-designed
banks, a tight arc, and good road traction will
mean a greater angle of lean. You should be on
the sharpest angle at the tightest part of the
turn.

As you begin your arc, raise the inside pedal
to its highest position and stand on your outside leg, with the knee slightly bent. This will
place your weight on the outside pedal, to
lower your center of gravity and increase tire
traction. The faster you take the turn the harder
you will have to press on the outside pedal.

Some riders point the inside knee into the
turn, maintaining that the extended knee increases stability and the turning force by catching the wind. Extending the knee is a matter of
individual preference.

If you feel that you are going too fast, resist

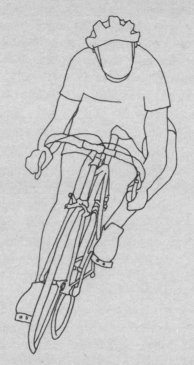

Figure 19   Leaning into a Turn

the urge to apply the brakes. Instead, lower
your outside hip while bending the outside
knee and rotating it into the turn. Although the
back wheel may slip or skid, your chances of
coming out of the turn will be greater than if
you had braked.

4. *Recovery:* Once you are past the tightest part
of the turn, gradually decrease the lean and

prepare yourself for the instant that you can resume pedaling. If there is another turn ahead, try to pedal fast between the two turns when your bike is passing through the vertical position.

Common beginners' mistakes include changing the line, braking, excessive leaning or pedaling too far into the turn, and catching the inside pedal on the road. Improved cornering skills come with increased confidence and are obtained only with experience. Practice cornering in residential neighborhoods during hours when traffic is at a minimum.

HILL CLIMBING

Cycling uphill is the hardest part of biking, and requires special riding techniques. To bike up a long hill you must alternate periods of sitting with periods of standing off the saddle. When you stand up to cycle, the entire body weight is put onto the forward pedal. Correct form involves "rocking" the bike from side to side so the pedal is positioned directly below the body. Though the frame may rock from side to side, it is important that the wheels follow a straight line. The hands must pull down on the top of the brake lever posts to increase the force transmitted through the pedals.

Figure 20   Standing to Pedal Uphill

When approaching a long, steep climb, stay
in gear and start standing as you reach the base of
the hill. When cadence can no longer be maintained, sit down, downshift, pedal several revolutions while sitting, and resume the standing position. Sprint for several revolutions to regain the
momentum lost during the shift. Repeat this routine until you are over the top of the hill.

It is important to realize that the bike has a
tendency to "slide" backward several inches each

time you get off the seat. This can be minimized by resisting the desire to lunge into the first downstroke, but rather gradually increasing the force on the pedals.

Pedaling off the saddle uses different muscles than in ordinary cycling posture, and allows for maximum oxygen intake. Runners often prefer standing because it puts strain on the muscles that have been strengthened by running. Experts do not agree whether standing or sitting is the most efficient way to bike uphill. Some great racers have been known for their standing technique, while others rarely left the saddle. Experts agree on one fact only: the best way to improve your hill-climbing ability is to lose weight. You will probably find that weight loss alone will improve your uphill cycling more than anything else.

4

MAINTAINING FITNESS

Biking for health and well-being is enhanced by a fitness lifestyle that prepares your body for stress and protects it from undue strain.

Proper nutrition will keep your energy level at its peak. Wise precautions will prevent injuries and correct treatment will speed their recovery. Monitoring your body for symptoms of overtraining will keep you from pushing beyond reasonable limits.

The key is knowing what works best for you—hearing what your body is telling you, and then following that message.

Remember that your body is a machine. Keep all the parts in good working order and you will be able to operate at peak level.

NUTRITION

The body needs fuel to keep going. Energy is produced through the body's metabolism of food. The body converts carbohydrates into glycogen, which is used to sustain daily activity and is stored in the muscles for "hard" times. When we exercise, glycogen reserves are converted to ATP (adenosine triphosphate). The breaking of ATP's molecular bonds releases energy, which the muscles use for motion. After our glycogen reserves are depleted, the body metabolizes fat and, to some extent, protein, for additional energy.

A well-balanced diet should include six essential nutrients: carbohydrates, fats, protein, water, vitamins, and minerals.

CARBOHYDRATES

Carbohydrates are an immediate energy source for all types of exercise. To maintain the optimum energy supply, your diet should contain 60 to 70 percent carbohydrates, with the percentage increasing prior to events requiring muscular endurance.

Atoms of carbon, hydrogen, and oxygen combine to form carbohydrates, which are called simple sugars in their most basic chemical structure. There are three kinds of carbohydrates: monosaccharides, disaccharides, and polysaccharides. Each form of carbohydrate is distinguished by the number of simple sugars it contains within the molecule. Glucose—a monosaccharide, also called blood sugar—is found as a natural substance in our food, and is produced through the digestion of more complicated carbohydrates. The major types of disaccharides are sucrose, found in brown sugar and honey; lactose, found in its natural form as a milk sugar; and maltose, found in malt products. Complex carbohydrates (polysaccharides) are the main source of energy for runners. They are commonly found in pasta, corn, bread, potatoes, flour, rice, and bran.

Complex carbohydrates are a better energy source than simple carbohydrates, because they are absorbed more slowly into the system and ensure a slow-burning, efficient form of energy.

When the muscles run out of glycogen, the blood-sugar level begins to drop. Muscles burn, fatigue, and cramp up. Further lowering of blood sugar leads to irritability, dizziness, nausea, loss of coordination, and ultimate collapse. Long-distance cyclists refer to this condition as "bonking," and marathon runners call it "hitting the wall." Some cyclists may develop hypoglycemia (low blood sugar) after eating large amounts of carbohydrates within 45 minutes to an hour before a race. Therefore, avoid sugar one hour before or during a race lasting more than two hours.

Endurance athletes practice "carbohydrate loading," which is accomplished by increasing the amount of complex carbohydrates in the diet for three days preceding a race. Carbohydrate loading and depletion came into vogue in the late '70s to help athletes cope with the increased energy demands of longer races, particularly marathons. It was believed that if you depleted your supply of stored carbohydrates in the beginning of the week before a race, you could trick your body into overloading on complex carbohydrates at the end of the week. However, recent findings indicate that your capacity for carbohydrate storage is not significantly increased by depletion. In fact, the depletion phase alters body chemistry and blood-sugar levels and induces fatigue, dizziness, irritability, and lethargy. Therefore, maintain a consistently healthy carbohydrate intake and practice carbohydrate loading when appropriate.

As race day approaches, maintain normal food volume and increase the proportion of complex carbohydrates. Do not overeat close to the start of the race, because any digestion occuring during the race will divert blood to the stomach that is needed in the muscles.

Consistent overeating of carbohydrates will not give you more energy. Rather, the unused quantities will be deposited under the skin in the form of adipose tissue—fat!

FATS

Fats are a secondary energy-producing nutrient, found primarily in vegetable oil, meat, dairy products, nuts, and egg yolks. Fat should account for no more than 15 percent of your daily food intake.

Body fat is the primary source of energy in the late stages of endurance events, when muscles have been depleted of glycogen. A well-trained athlete can store glycogen in the muscles in a quantity that is equal to roughly 2,700 calories. During heavy exertion, this storage is depleted in under three hours. The additional energy is supplied by metabolism of fat and protein. This is done with great difficulty by the untrained athlete, but one's ability can be improved with endurance training.

One pound of fat supplies twice the number of calories (twice the amount of energy) as one pound of glycogen. However, the conversion of fat is much slower than the metabolism of carbohydrates.

Fats carry four essential fat-soluble vitamins—A, D, E, and K. Fat cushions the internal organs from shock, and provides insulation against cold. Excess layers of fat under the skin prevent dissipation of heat, and may cause the body to overheat during physical exercise. Excess fat will also limit the amount of oxygen that the blood can supply to the muscles.

WATER

Water is essential for metabolism. It also regulates body temperature and cleanses the system. Your body will tell you how much water it needs. Drink as much as you desire, since any excess will be secreted in the urine.

Excessive water loss leads to dehydration and subsequent chemical imbalance within the body. During sustained exercise it is extremely important to drink large amounts of water to keep the body cool, prevent dehydration and heat exhaustion, and aid in flushing lactic acid from the muscles.

Drink lots of water before, during, and after a race, even if you have to force yourself to do so.

PROTEIN

The structural material of our cells is composed predominantly of protein. Protein cannot be stored in the body, and any excess is broken down in the liver and secreted. This is why we need a constant supply to maintain good health.

Since the training process involves a "breaking down" and rebuilding of muscle cells, it is a common misconception that athletes should increase the amount of protein in their diets. However, nutritionists agree that this is not neces-

sary, since a well-rounded diet will supply adequate amounts of protein to rebuild muscle cells.

Limit protein to 10 percent of your food
intake. Meat, eggs, cheese, fish, and yogurt are
good sources of protein.

VITAMINS

Vitamins are chemical compounds that activate and regulate the flow of enzymes during
metabolism. We must obtain all of our vitamins
from our diet, since the human body is incapable
of synthesizing them. It is extremely important to
eat a well-rounded diet containing adequate
amounts of fresh fruit and vegetables.

Water-soluble vitamins—B-complex and C—
are carried in the blood plasma to all parts of the
body, and excess amounts are secreted in the
urine. Since water-soluble vitamins are not stored
in the body, we require a daily intake to maintain
fitness. B-complex vitamins are abundant in meat,
eggs, and milk. Vitamin C is plentiful in citrus fruits,
tomatoes, and raw green vegetables. Because
these vitamins are dissolved in water, excess
cooking of vegetables robs them of their nutrients.

Fat-soluble vitamins—A, D, E, and K—are
dissolved, transported, and stored in body fat.
Excess amounts are not secreted, and can become toxic if too much collects in the body.

Vitamin A is found in dark green, orange, or

yellow vegetables, and meats; K is found in green leafy vegetables and egg yolks; E is found in wheat germ, whole grains, and some green vegetables.

Much controversy exists among nutritionists as to whether an athlete-in-training requires higher doses of vitamins. A multiple vitamin and mineral supplement is recommended as a cheap form of insurance.

MINERALS

About 4 percent of the body's weight is composed of metallic elements that are collectively called minerals. Minerals serve as important parts of enzymes that regulate cellular metabolism. They activate reactions that release energy during the breakdown of carbohydrates, fats, and proteins. Minerals are essential for synthesizing glycogen from glucose, fat from fatty acids and glycerol, and protein from amino acids.

Minerals are classified as "major" or "trace," depending on their quantities in the body. Major minerals include sodium, potassium, chlorine, magnesium, phosphorus, sulfur, and calcium. Trace minerals include aluminum, copper, iodine, manganese, fluorine, nickel, tin, cobalt, and zinc.

Large amounts of minerals are lost through perspiration, and must be replaced in adequate quantities during and after exercise.

Sodium (salt), potassium, and chlorine are collectively called "electrolytes." Excessive loss of electrolytes impairs heat tolerance and exercise performance, and may lead to cramps, heat exhaustion, or heat stroke.

Salt regulates the body's water content. It is not uncommon for an endurance athlete to lose up to 10 pounds of water containing 0.3 ounces of salt. There is an immediate need to replenish this loss. Endurance athletes actually "train" their bodies to retain larger amounts of salt, to meet increased demands. We unconsciously increase our salt intake when the need exists. It is available in meat, fish, chicken, grains, and nuts.

It is a dangerous myth that salt supplement tablets should be taken before and during an event. Actually, salt tablets can induce further deterioration of our vital salt balance. Salt tablets will raise the salt level in our blood, drawing water from the muscles to dilute the salt concentration, and further depriving the muscles of much needed water. Excessive salt intake will increase urination and further contribute to dehydration.

If you remain unconvinced about the hazards of salt intake during a race, a safer alternative to tablets is a solution of 1/3 teaspoon of salt mixed with one quart of water.

Excessive perspiration can also lead to a potassium or magnesium deficiency. Potassium is released into the bloodstream and plays an important role in delaying muscle fatigue. Bananas

SOURCES OF MINERALS IN FOODS*

CALCIUM	IRON	MAGNESIUM	PHOSPHORUS	SODIUM	POTASSIUM
Milk	Meat	Nuts	Dried peas	Vegetables	Citrus fruits
Hard cheese	Turnip greens	Soybeans	Dried beans	Fruits	Vegetables
Turnip greens	Kale	Wheat germ	Brussels sprouts	Grains	
Broccoli	Chard	Spinach	Sweet corn		
Cauliflower	Lettuce		Peas		
Spinach	Cabbage				
Celery	Spinach				
Carrots	Mustard greens				
String beans	Dried peas				
Raw cabbage	Eggs				
Peas					

*Vegetables, fruits, milk, eggs, and whole-grain cereals are excellent sources of the other trace elements.

are recommended as an easily digested, highly concentrated source of potassium.

Several electrolyte "replacement" drinks claim to instantly replenish the electrolytes and sugar that is lost in sustained endurance exercise. However, sugar and salt will actually draw water and blood to the stomach for digestion—robbing the muscles of water and pushing you closer to dehydration. These drinks also remain in the stomach for too long before they are digested, and thus cannot offer "instant pick-up." If you do decide to drink electrolyte replacement, experiment before the day of the race to make sure that it works for you.

Iron is another mineral that is lost through excessive perspiration. This important mineral combines with protein to form hemoglobin, which is the red substance in blood that carries oxygen to the muscles. Nutritionists claim that up to 40 percent of American women in their child-bearing years suffer from iron deficiency. In severe cases this leads to anemia accompanied by a run-down, fatigued feeling that will affect athletic performance. Women are advised to make sure that they have an adequate daily supply of iron, which is found in red meat, liver, green-leaved vegetables, raisins, and prunes.

There is no evidence to date proving that increased mineral intake will "boost" performance—although basic requirements must be supplied and maintained in any training program.

INJURY PREVENTION AND TREATMENT

All athletes, regardless of the sport they are involved in, will periodically be subject to sports-related injuries. Tennis players develop "tennis elbow," baseball players often get hit with a hard ball, basketball players commonly sprain fingers, while injuries to football players or runners are well known to us all.

Biking is no exception; it is not safer or more dangerous than any other sport, and it too has its share of injuries. Some cycling-related injuries are common to all aerobic activities, while others are unique to the sport. Since there are many good books available on the subject of general sport injuries, our discussion will focus on injuries unique to cycling.

ROAD RASH

The most common cycling-related injuries are the direct result of an accident or "spill." Road rash is the cyclists' term for lacerations that result when the body is thrown off the bike and onto the road. Although it is not a rash in the conventional sense of the word, the injury is usually more painful and severe than that associated with a skin rash.

Falling off the bike is inevitable. The first thing to do after a fall is thoroughly check the damaged area. If you are not near a first-aid station, and if the injury is not severe, you should rinse the wound with water from your water bottle. Rinsing away surface dirt and gravel is necessary to reduce the risk of secondary infection.

Deeply imbedded dirt must be scrubbed out with soap and running water. The area should be scrubbed vigorously since any dirt particles left in the wound will lead to infection. This should be done as soon as you have the facilities, because the wound will start to swell and become very sensitive in one to two hours. Apply ice directly or in a towel or ice-pack, to numb the area and make the scrubbing job less painful. Scrubbing may still be painful, but it will greatly speed up the healing process. Don't be alarmed if scrubbing makes the wound ooze bright red blood, since this bleeding will flush and help cleanse the wound.

If hydrogen peroxide is available, pour it over the wound, dry off excess by patting with a sterile gauze pad, and cover the raw area with a petroleum-based ointment. Neosporin is an over-the-counter ointment which will prevent a scab from forming. Change the dressing at least once a day and keep the wound moist with Neosporin. This is important, because a scab will usually prolong the time it takes before you are able to ride again.

Watch for signs of infection such as swelling,

secretion of pus, redness extending to surrounding skin, and excessive warmth or tenderness. If the wound appears to be infected, it is wise to see a doctor, who will probably prescribe antibiotics to fight the infection. It is advised to see a doctor if you have not had a tetanus shot within the last five years, regardless of the severity of the wound.

SADDLE SORES

This "injury" is probably one that every cyclist experiences at least once in his or her biking career. If you are a new cyclist, you are probably more aware of this problem than you care to be.

In its milder stages, saddle soreness causes discomfort and a "forced" lay-off from riding. In more severe cases it will result in the formation of blisters, boils, and open wounds. The pain from open sores is excruciating and cannot be done justice in a brief verbal description. Saddle sores are very frustrating because, aside from being unable to sit on your seat, you will probably feel full of energy and eager to ride.

Cleanliness is very important to prevent infection of saddle sores, since they are irritated by sweat and bacteria growth. The chamois lining in the cycling shorts should be washed after each ride to prevent bacteria and dirt from penetrating the sores.

To reduce friction and irritation, you can apply Vaseline or similar water-based lubricants (Noxzema is good) to the buttocks and genital areas. Although this will eliminate much of the friction, cleanliness must be maintained. Rubbing down the tender area with alcohol before and after a long ride will help prevent infection and is believed to have a toughening effect on the skin.

Unfortunately, the best way to prevent saddle sores is to toughen up the vulnerable area by spending long hours in the saddle. If you think that you are being led into a "vicious cycle" or a "Catch-22," you are right—to date no fool-proof method of preventing saddle sores has been found.

Sores are sometimes caused by irritation from the seams in cycling shorts or underpants. This is easily rectified by switching to seamless shorts made specifically to prevent this problem (see the section on cycling shorts, page 20). A leather saddle will eventually mold itself to your shape and become the most comfortable saddle that you can own. Experienced cyclists sometimes use a good-quality saddle for many years, transferring a broken-in saddle from one bike to another. Be forewarned that a leather saddle requires roughly 1,000 miles of riding before it starts to become "comfortable."

A saddle that is either too high or low or tilted wrong will contribute to the formation of saddle sores. See pages 9-13 and experiment with saddle adjustment if you think that incorrect saddle positioning is causing your discomfort.

It may soothe your pain to know that everyone who cycles for fitness and spends long hours in the saddle must learn to cope with this problem. A well-designed and properly adjusted saddle, padded cycling shorts, and routine cleanliness will make the problem of saddle sores one that can be easily dealt with.

NUMBNESS

Numbness is the result of compressing a nerve for an extended period of time. It may occur in the hands, crotch, or feet while cycling.

The hands may numb in the wrist or fourth and pinky finger when a nerve is compressed between a bone and the handlebars. Cyclists who neglect the early signs of numbness and let the situation deteriorate have reported numbness lasting days or even weeks afterwards. The problem is usually remedied with cycling gloves that are well padded in the palm, by wrapping the handlebars with protective cushioning material, and by switching positions on the handlebars every few minutes. Alternate between the three basic handlebar positions described on pages 32-36. This is probably the most effective corrective measure, with the extra benefit of changing your body angle, which will also delay fatigue and muscle cramping in the neck, shoulder, and back.

Numbness in the crotch is an experience that is more startling than serious. It usually results from an upward tilt of the saddle pressing against the crotch, and is further aggravated by a saddle that is too high. Moving forward and backward on the saddle and occasionally pedaling while standing will ease the pressure in this area.

Numbness in the feet accompanied by a burning sensation is caused by the pressure of the pedal against the sole of the foot. Poor circulation is often the cause of foot numbness. Most cycling shoes have a hard sole and offer very little cushioning. Common remedies include resilient insoles and thick socks. Pedal straps that are too tight will also cause numbness and must be loosened periodically to allow increased blood circulation.

KNEE INJURIES

Knee injuries are more prevalent than any other chronic sports-related injury. Although the knee is the largest joint in the body, it is also one of the weakest from a biomechanical standpoint. This is partially because the bones in the knee never achieve more than partial contact throughout the entire range of motion from flexion (bending) to extension (straightening). There is no "ball and socket" construction as there is in other structurally sound joints such as the shoulder and hip.

The knee is composed of three moving bones: the thigh bone (femur), lower leg bone (tibia), and the knee cap (patella). Three major muscle groups move the knee joint and provide the forces that spin the pedals. The hamstrings and calf muscles contract to bend the knee while the quadriceps straighten the leg. The knee is designed for bending only and allows for no sideways movement.

Overuse injuries associated with the knee include bursitis, tendinitis, and chondromalacia.

Bursitis

The knee is surrounded by eighteen pockets (bursas) of fluid that act as lubricants between the moving bones. The bursas can become inflamed and irritated by general overuse, particularly when pushing too high a gear. Chronic bursitis may cause swelling and fluid collection within the bursas. The best treatment for mild bursitis is rest from cycling, application of ice, and aspirin. Chronic bursitis accompanied by large fluid accumulation in the bursas must be treated professionally.

Tendinitis

The knee is surrounded by numerous tendons that can become inflamed from overuse. The most common forms of tendinitis experienced by cyclists involve the tendons directly below the kneecap (patellar tendinitis) and the tendons to the outside rear of the knee (popliteal tendinitis). Popliteal tendinitis often results from a saddle that is too high, causing extreme extension of the knee.

The treatment for all forms of tendinitis is rest, application of ice immediately after the ride, and aspirin. Tendinitis can usually be differentiated from other forms of knee injuries by the fact that the pain slowly subsides after a 15- to 20-minute warm-up ride.

Chondromalacia

This condition is a roughening and disintegration of the undersurface of the kneecap and the cartilage surfaces that separate the thigh and lower leg bones. The undersurface of the kneecap and the adjacent cartilage surfaces normally glide like ice sliding on ice. With chondromalacia, commonly known as "runner's knee," it feels as if sand has been thrown in between the gliding surfaces. Eventually the grinding action will wear down the bone endings and related cartilage surfaces. Early symptoms are pain under the knee-cap and a grating sensation.

Chondromalacia is probably the severest and most disabling knee injury that a cyclist may experience. It is a difficult problem to treat and should be dealt with before it progresses to a chronic disability, because there is no satisfactory cure for it. Usually, the condition is caused by incorrect saddle height or shoe/cleat position. Orthotics can often improve foot abnormalities by stabilizing the foot.

Treatment for chondromalacia includes rest from cycling, application of ice to reduce swelling, and aspirin. Once the pain is reduced and the cause is diagnosed and corrected, a program of weight training to strengthen the quadriceps and calf and hamstring muscles should be initiated.

SYMPTOMS OF OVERTRAINING

You must listen to your body signals and give yourself a chance to rest between hard workouts. Training benefits are maximized with sufficient recovery time.

The symptoms of overtraining are initially mild and may seem unimportant. However, if you ignore these symptoms and allow them to persist or intensify, you increase the risk of injury and an extended lay-up.

Since any of the following symptoms could appear regardless of the training effort, a combination of three or more symptoms is an almost sure sign of overtraining. If you suspect symptoms of overtraining, schedule easier workouts or rest completely until you're back to "normal."

Increase in Morning Pulse Rate

This is the most widely recognized symptom of overtraining. Measure your pulse rate upon awakening, before getting out of bed. Find the artery in the neck, just below the chin, and count the number of beats in a 10-second interval. Multiply this number by 6 to calculate your pulse rate. An increase of eight to 10 beats per minute is a good indication that your body is over-stressed. Do not resume workouts until your morning pulse drops back to normal.

General Feeling of Fatigue

If you have a lingering feeling of tiredness, your body is trying to tell you that it cannot keep up with your level of training.

Delayed Recovery Time

Be alert for sore muscles that take longer than usual to heal. Muscle soreness usually sets in 36 to 48 hours after a workout, and should not remain for more than two days. Muscles may be exercised moderately when they are sore and tender, but hard workouts should be avoided. Ease off training if the muscles have not recovered after several days.

Sleep Irregularities

Called "depression insomnia" by running authority Dr. George Sheehan, this symptom is characterized by falling asleep early in the evening but awakening early in the morning with a feeling of energetic uneasiness, and tiring at midday. You should be getting a sound night's sleep, waking at your usual time, and feeling refreshed and eager to work out.

Mental Exhaustion

Irritability, apathy, and moodiness are psychological indicators of overtraining. Loss of motivation is a definite warning signal. Training should be an activity that you look forward to, offering you excitement and enjoyment.

Loss of Appetite and Weight

A significant decrease in appetite or an unusual drop in weight can mean that the body is buckling under the work load and trying to "rebel" against further stress.

Lowered Body Resistance

Fever blisters, headaches, upset stomach, and colds are all symptoms of excessive stress.

5 THE TRAINING PROGRAM

To improve and sustain good biking ability, complement your workout routines with a well-rounded program that includes resistance training, stretching in the warm-up and cool-down phases of every ride, and a wise combination of LSD, interval, HIT, and wind-load simulator workouts.

RESISTANCE TRAINING

Cyclists are usually well developed in the lower body, but need to develop strength and mobility in the lower back, neck, arms, and shoulders. Resistance training, commonly known as weight training, is exercise designed to increase muscle strength and endurance. Although weight training is not a substitute for a fitness program based on cycling, it can be very useful in developing upper body strength and increasing flexibility.

Research has not proved that weight training will reduce the chance of injury, but a strong upper body will give you better control of your bike and reduce the risk of an accident. Upper body strength will improve your performance during acceleration, sprinting, hill climbing, and riding in strong crosswinds.

Weight training can develop muscle bulk, strength, or endurance, depending on the type and amount of exercise that is involved. A program of few repetitions with heavy weights will develop muscle bulk. A program of many repetitions with lighter weights will develop strength and cardiovascular endurance, increase blood supply to the muscles, and produce only a small increase in muscle fiber diameter.

Weight training can be accomplished by having your body offer its own resistance, by employing free weights such as barbells and dumbbells, or by using fixed and progressive resistance such as that provided on Nautilus and Universal machines.

Experts do not agree on the actual aerobic benefits associated with weight training. However, there is a consensus that "circuit weight training" is the best form of resistance training for cyclists. This consists of a series of exercises, each done for a short period at a separate "station," with a brief rest between stations. A circuit is considered complete when you have exercised at all of the stations in the circuit.

Circuit training will develop and tone your muscles, and is an excellent supplement to the aerobic workout that is achieved on the bike. It will not develop muscle bulk, which is a concern to many cyclists. Circuit training concentrates on the upper body, stimulating muscle fibers that are not commonly used in cycling, increasing blood supply to the muscles, and resulting in overall improved endurance.

The following circuit program is based on body resistance and free-weight exercises. It is a circuit that can be easily set up at home with a $20 set of variable resistance dumbbells. The circuit includes six stations. A total of 20 minutes should be devoted to circuit training, two to three times a week. Always warm up your muscles and increase blood circulation by cycling on a wind-load simulator or taking a short jog.

Begin with weights that you can easily handle for 10 to 15 repetitions. Increase the weights on the dumbbells only after you are capable of handling 15 repetitions comfortably. Don't sacrifice form or technique or risk injury by training with weights that are too heavy. Rest between each station for as long as it takes you to complete the exercise at the preceding station. Repeat the circuit as many times as you possibly can, but do not exceed one half hour of weight training in one day.

Concentrate on the contraction and relaxation phase of each repetition, and use your muscles throughout the full range of motion. Don't let gravity pull the weight, or your body weight, back down.

Dumbbell Curls

This is the best exercise for the biceps—the muscles in the upper arms that look so impressive when flexed. Hold your body erect, palms facing front, and slowly lift the weights until they are at shoulder level. Slowly lower the weights, and feel the pressure throughout the entire movement. Keep your elbows against the sides of your body while performing this exercise.

Figure 21
Dumbell Curls

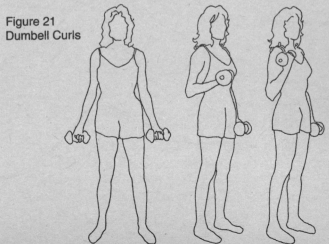

Bent Knee Sit-Ups

This strengthens the abdominal muscles. Lie
on your back with your knees bent, feet together,
and hands clasped together under your neck.
Tuck your chin down to your chest and slowly curl
your torso upward until your chest touches your
knees. Slowly return to your original position.
Repeat this exercise 20 to 30 times before going
on to the next station. It may be easier for you to
perform this exercise with someone holding
down your ankles.

Figure 22   Bent Knee Sit-Ups

Triceps Extension

This exercise should be done with one dumbbell held with both hands behind the neck. Begin with the elbows pointing upward, as close to the head as possible, and the dumbbell touching the back between the shoulders. Lift the weight to the highest position, concentrating on keeping the elbows close to the head. Slowly lower the weight behind the back, using the elbows as if they were stationary hinges. This is an excellent exercise for developing the triceps (muscles in the back of the arms) and the deltoid (shoulder) muscles.

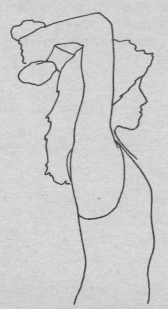

Figure 23 Triceps Extension

Push-Ups

This is one of the best exercises for developing
upper body strength. They should be performed
in two variations. With hands placed at
shoulder width, you will develop strength in the
triceps and deltoid muscles. Push-ups performed
with hands spread roughly 10 inches wider than
shoulder width will develop the pectoral muscles
(chest) and trapezius muscles (upper back).
Support your body on the palms of your hands
and on your toes. Maintain a straight line from your
neck to your heels. Slowly lower your body until
your chest almost touches the floor, and then
push yourself up to the starting position. Practice
increasing the number of repetitions, up to 50.
Alternate the two push-up styles each time
around the circuit.

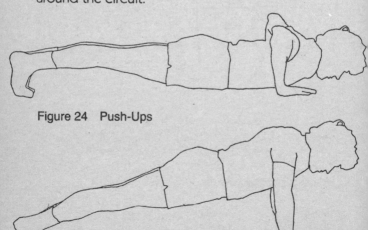

Figure 24   Push-Ups

Pectoral Raises

This is highly recommended for developing
the pectoral (upper chest) muscles. You will need
a bench and two dumbbells for the routine. Lie
on the bench with a dumbbell in each hand,
palms facing up, the weights held out at your
sides, parallel to the ground, and the elbows
slightly bent. Slowly raise the dumbbells until they
meet at a point directly over your chest. Gradually
lower the dumbbells to the starting position.

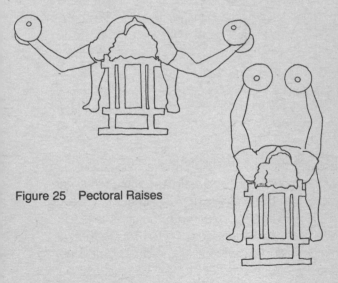

Figure 25   Pectoral Raises

Military Press

This is the single best exercise for developing
the shoulder muscles (deltoids) as well as the
muscles in the back, neck, and upper arms. Stand

Figure 26
Military Press

holding the weights slightly over your shoulders, with elbows bent and palms facing each other. Slowly lift the weights upward until the elbows are in a locked position with the arms extended overhead. Hold this position for two to three seconds and slowly lower the dumbbells back to shoulder height. Do not let the weights rest on your shoulders between repetitions.

The preceding exercises are a basic circuit program for resistance training, emphasizing upper body development. It is assumed that the lower body muscles will be sufficiently developed by cycling, although additional exercises may be added to the circuit if greater lower body strength is required.

STRETCHING

This is an important element in every fitness routine. Stretching increases your range of motion; loosens muscles, tendons, and ligaments; and heightens body awareness. It reduces tension and the risk of muscle strain, promotes circulation, and speeds recovery from minor muscle tears. Flexibility and resiliency decrease with age, so the older you are the more important stretching becomes.

All muscles work in pairs. As one muscle, the "agonist," contracts, the opposing muscle, or "antagonist," must extend and relax. It is important to stretch against both muscles, so each muscle in the pair is contracted and extended. The following series of stretches is designed to accomplish this task.

Each exercise should be done slowly and gradually, extending the muscle to the threshold of pain and maintaining that position for a minimum of 60 seconds. Do not bounce through the stretch, as this causes micro-tears in muscle tissue.

Breathe rhythmically throughout the routine. Exhale going into the stretch, and inhale as you relax the muscles.

Devote at least 10 minutes before and after every ride to complete the following eight basic stretches.

Head Rolls

This is a basic stretch for the neck muscles. Rotate your head slowly, carefully controlling its movement. Keep the back straight at all times. Stop and hold the stretch at any point that feels tight.

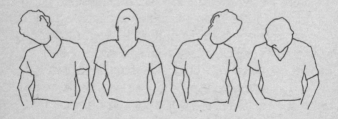

Figure 27   Head Rolls

Toe Touches

This stretches the hamstrings, backs of the knees, and the back. Slowly bend forward from the hips, rolling down one vertebra at a time. Keep the knees very slightly bent, to avoid undue

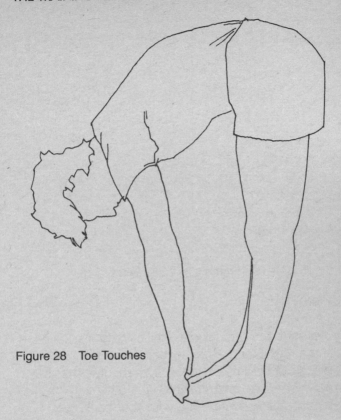

Figure 28   Toe Touches

stress on the back. Relax the upper back, arms, and shoulders.

Maintain your position at the threshold of pain for 60 seconds. You will find that the pain subsides and you can further extend the stretch after holding the position for approximately 20 seconds.

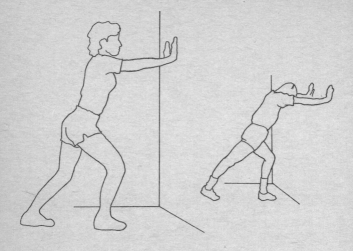

Figure 29   Wall Pushes

Wall Push

This stretches the calves, Achilles tendons, and ankles. Stand a few inches from a wall and place both palms on the wall, at shoulder height. Bend one knee and straighten the other leg, extending it in a straight line with your back. Lean into the wall by moving your hips forward. You will feel a pull in the calf and the front of the ankle. Hold this position for 60 seconds.

To stretch the Achilles tendon, slightly bend the outstretched leg at the knee. Always keep both feet flat on the floor and your back straight. Extend the leg back as far as necessary to feel the pull in the calf and Achilles tendon.

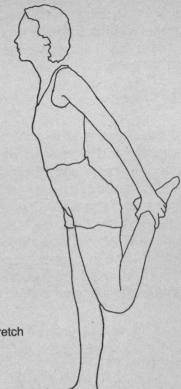

Figure 30   Quad Stretch

Quad Stretch

This stretches the quadriceps—the main muscle
group used in cycling. Put one hand against the
wall for balance. Bend the knee and lift your
foot behind you, pulling up with your hand.
Bring the heel of the foot as close to the buttocks
as possible and hold the position at the point of

pain. Gradually increase the stretch as the pain decreases and the contraction becomes easier. You should feel the stretch in the muscles directly above the knee.

Groin Stretch

To stretch the groin, sit with the soles of your feet together and knees apart. Hold the soles together with both hands. Bring the feet in as close as possible to the groin, and try to lower your knees to the ground. Slowly lean forward from the hips, lowering your head toward your feet until you feel slight discomfort. Try to hold the feet as close to the groin as possible. Do not bend from the head and shoulders, as this will put undue pressure on the lower back.

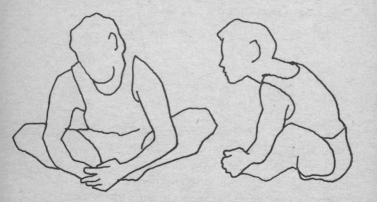

Figure 31   Groin Stretch

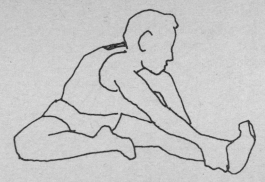

Figure 32   Hamstring Stretch

Hamstring Stretch

This stretches the hamstrings, lower back, and groin areas. Sit with one leg extended straight out, with the toes pointing upward. Bend the other leg so the sole of the foot is resting against the inner thigh of the straight leg. Bend from the hip, toward the foot of the extended leg, and try to touch your toes. If you cannot reach the toes, hold the leg with both hands as close to the ankle as possible. Keep the quadriceps, ankle, and toes relaxed. Switch legs and repeat in the same manner.

Side Stretch

Stand with legs straight and spread a comfortable distance apart. Reach down one side of your body, as if to touch your foot. Do not raise

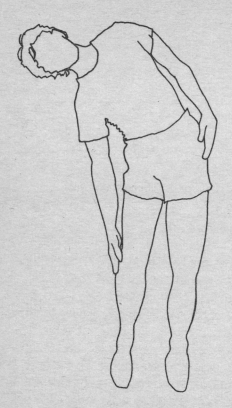

Figure 33 Side Stretch

the heel of the foot opposite the hand that is
reaching for the foot. You should feel a stretching
from your shoulder blade to your hips.

For an advanced version of this stretch, reach
for your foot with the opposite hand extended
over your head.

Figure 34   Knee Squats

Knee Squats

This is a required stretch for the front of the
ankles, Achilles tendons, knees, and lower back.
Squat down with feet flat on the floor, toes
pointed slightly inward, and heels one foot apart.
Keep the knees spread wider than the shoulder
span. Totally relax all of your muscles, and lower
the buttocks as far as possible. To increase the
stretch in the groin, place your elbows against the

inside of both knees and gently apply pressure outward, spreading the knees further apart.

Be cautious with squats if you are plagued by knee problems.

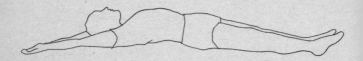

Extension Stretch

This is excellent for both stretching and relaxing the entire body. Lie on the floor with your body fully extended and your hands stretched overhead. Maintain a flat back and press down with the small of the back. Point your toes and reach out with your fingers, stretching the torso as far as possible. Stretch for 10 seconds and relax, repeating this motion six times. This stretches the rib cage, abdomen, spine, shoulders, arms, legs, ankles, and feet.

*Stretch immediately after a hard workout to prevent muscles from tightening, minimize muscle discomfort, and promote a speedier recovery.

The key to effective stretching is relaxed muscles, relaxed breathing, and a relaxed mind.

WARM-UP AND COOL-DOWN

The preceding stretching exercises are to be incorporated into every warm-up and cool-down session.

THE WARM-UP

This is an integral phase of every workout, and of major importance before intervals or short races. Indulging in strenuous exercise without adequate warm-up time will lead to injuries and far longer recuperation times. A sufficient warm-up session significantly reduces the chance of injury, as it gradually increases stress on the muscles, increases heart and breathing rates, and elevates muscle temperature.

Begin each workout with the series of stretching exercises described on pages 101-110. Usually, 10 to 15 minutes is adequate. Cyclists can warm up on the bike with five to 10 minutes of pedaling at speed.

The length of the warm-up period should be increased with the intensity of the workout. Warming up becomes less important on long races, when you have time to warm up in the early stages of the event. Energy, which will be needed during the final miles, should be conserved.

THE COOL-DOWN

The cool-down is as important as the warm-up, but for a different reason. Cooling down is necessary to minimize recovery time between workouts. Light exercise helps reduce the lactic acid level in our muscles and prevents it from flowing into the stomach, where it may cause nausea and possibly vomiting. The continued circulation also aids in bringing the blood from the working muscles back to the heart.

The cool-down should be a gradual reduction of exertion and movement, lasting 10 to 15 minutes. A conscientious cool-down session will help reduce soreness in the muscles that many athletes feel the morning after a hard workout.

12-WEEK TRAINING PROGRAM

This program is a model for cyclists who wish to improve long-distance touring or racing techniques as well as for those interested in developing and maintaining fitness. It is general in nature and should be modified to your individual needs and fitness level. Use the program as a guide to help you develop your own tailor-made routine.

THE TRAINING PROGRAM   113

The 12-week schedule is divided into three four-week phases. Each phase has a specific goal. As you progress you will build endurance, strength, speed, and stamina. Your personal program may deviate from the following in workout days and distances, but each phase should be oriented to the tasks presented here. The program assumes that even the novice can ride six slow miles, and it is from this point that you begin.

Phase 1

The first four weeks should be devoted to building basic endurance and mastering biking fundamentals (see Chapter 3 on body position, shifting gears, pedaling, and braking). Try to ride on flat terrain so you can concentrate on riding basics without putting undue stress on your body. Maintain a steady pace as much as possible, and raise your heart rate to roughly 70 percent of its maximum. Listen to your body—it will tell you at what speed you should be riding. Avoid pushing too high gears or overstressing yourself to the point of injury.

You are building your aerobic foundation in this phase. Most rides will be LSD, but experiment with one HIT ride a week during the latter part of this phase. Do not exceed more than four days of riding a week even if you feel that you have the energy to do so. Alternatively, increase the pace or distance of your daily rides if you feel you can

handle additional exertion. Don't forget the warm-
up and cool-down, especially in conjunction with
HIT rides.

Phase 2

This is the time to concentrate on building
strength and speed. Before beginning phase 2
you should be capable of riding 20 miles at
roughly 70 percent of your maximum heart rate,
and demonstrating proficiency in the cycling
fundamentals stressed in phase 1. During this
phase you will devote a minimum of one day a
week to HIT training and one day to interval (INT)
workouts. Gradually increase the time and mileage
of these strengthening workouts, since they form
the basis for competitive cycling and increased
cardiovascular fitness.

Begin experimenting with "pushing" your
body beyond its current physical limits. Don't
forget to alternate hard and easy workout days, to
allow your body to adapt and achieve the maximum benefits from the training effect.

Phase 3

This sharpening phase brings together endurance, strength, and speed to produce stamina.
You should incorporate advanced skills into HIT
and interval rides two to three times a week, and
include at least one LSD ride. Most important to

12-WEEK TRAINING FOR 50-MILE RIDE

	WEEK	SUN.	MON.	TUE.	WED.	THUR.	FRI.	SAT.	TOTAL
INITIAL ENDURANCE	1	6/LSD	R	6/LSD	R	6/LSD	R	10/LSD	28
	2	6/LSD	R	10/LSD	R	6/LSD	R	10/LSD	32
	3	6/LSD	R	10/LSD	3/HIT	R	6/LSD	15/LSD	40
	4	R	10/LSD	R	4/HIT	R	6/LSD	20/LSD	37
BUILD STRENGTH	5	8/LSD	6/HIT	R	10/LSD	4/INT	R	25/LSD	53
	6	10/LSD	4/INT	R	10/LSD	6/HIT	R	25/LSD	50
	7	6/LSD	R	3/INT	6/HIT	R	4/INT	30/LSD	49
	8	10/LSD	R	12/LSD	4/INT	R	10/HIT	35/LSD	71
SHARPEN SKILLS	9	R	20/LSD	14/HIT	15/LSD	6/INT	R	40/LSD	95
	10	20/LSD	R	10/HIT	R	8/INT	R	45/LSD	83
	11	20/LSD	R	15/HIT	25/LSD	10/INT	R	45/LSD	115
	12	20/LSD	R	20/HIT	25/LSD	10/INT	R	50/LSD	125

competitive cyclists, this phase emphasizes hill
climbing and perfects riding a straight line and
cornering skills.

The 12-week program mixes hard workouts
(INT and HIT) with easy (LSD) rides of varying
duration and pace. As you being to understand
your fitness level and aerobic requirements, you
will discover your most efficient weekly cycling
regimen. Substitute indoor workouts on the wind-
load simulator (see pages 51–53) on days when
outdoor riding is inconvenient.

Suggested Reading

General

Ballantine, Richard. *Richard's Bicycling Book.* New York: Ballantine Books, 1978.

Delong, Fred. *Delong's Guide to Bicycles and Bicycling: The Art and Science.* Radnor, PA: Chilton, 1978.

Doughty, Tom. *The Complete Book of Long Distance and Competitive Cycling.* New York: Simon and Schuster, 1983.

The Editors of Bicycling Magazine. *Basic Riding Techniques.* Emmaus, PA: Rodale Press, 1979.

Hoyt, Creig S., and Julie Hoyt. *Cycling.* Dubuque, Iowa: Wm. C. Brown Publishers, 1984.

Kolin, Michael J. *Cycling for Sport.* Seattle, WA: Velosport Press, 1984.

Kolin, M., and D. de la Rosa. *The Custom Bicycle.* Emmaus, PA: Rodale Press, 1979.

Kolin, M., and D. de la Rosa. *The Ten Speed Bicycle.* Emmaus, PA: Rodale Press, 1979.

McCullagh, James C. *The Complete Bicycle Fitness Book.* New York: Warner Books, 1984.

Sloane, Eugene A. *The All New Complete Book of Bicycling.* New York: Simon and Schuster, 1980.

Wollenmuller, Franz. *How to Succeed at Cycling.* New York: Sterling Publishing Co., 1982.

Touring/Commuting

Allen, John S. *The Complete Book of Bicycle Commuting.* Emmaus, PA: Rodale Press, 1981.

Bike Touring. San Francisco, CA: Sierra Club Books, 1979.

Cuthbertson, Tom. *Bike Tripping.* Berkeley, CA: Ten Speed Press, 1972.

The Editors of Bicycling Magazine. *Best Bicycle Tours.* Emmaus, PA: Rodale Press, 1981.

―――. *Bicycle Commuting.* Emmaus, PA: Rodale Press, 1980.

Heilman, Gail. *The Complete Outfitting and Source Book for Bicycle Touring.* Marshall, CA: The Great Outdoors Trading Company, 1980.

Lieb, Thom. *Everybody's Book of Bicycle Riding.* Emmaus, PA: Rodale Press, 1981.

Tobey, P., and T. Tucker, eds. *Two Wheel Travel: Bicycle Camping and Travelling by Bike.* Mountain View, CA: World Publication, 1974.

Wilhelm, Tim, and Glenda Wilhelm. *The Bicycle Touring Book.* Emmaus, PA: Rodale Press, 1980.

Racing

All About Bicycle Racing. Mountain View, CA:
   World Publications, 1975.
Complete Bicycle Time Trialing Book. Mountain
   View, CA: World Publications, 1977.
Matheny, Fred. *Beginning Bicycle Racing.* Brattle-
   boro, VT: Velo-news, 1981.
Simes, Jack. *Ten Years of Championship Bicycle
   Racing.* Brattleboro, VT: Velo-news, 1983.
————. *Winning Bicycle Racing.* Chicago, IL: Con-
   temporary Books, Inc., 1976.

Maintenance/Repair

Brandt, Jobst. *The Bicycle Wheel.* Menlo Park, CA:
   Avocet, Inc., 1981.
Cuthbertson, Tom. *Anybody's Bike Book.* Berkeley,
   CA: Ten Speed Press, 1979.
The Editors of Bicycling Magazine. *Basic Bicycle
   Repair.* Emmaus, PA: Rodale Press, 1980.
Glenn, Harold T., and Clarence W. Coles. *Glenn's
   Complete Bicycle Manual.* New York: Crown
   Publishers, 1973.

Triathlon

Edwards, Sally. *Triathlon: A Triple Fitness Sport.*
   Chicago, IL: Contemporary Books, Inc., 1983.

Johnson, Bob, and Patricia Bragg. *The Complete Triathlon Swim, Bike and Run Distance Training Manual.* Santa Barbara, CA: Health Science Publications, 1982.

Perry, Paul. *Paul Perry's Complete Book of the Triathlon.* New York: Plume Books, 1983.

Sisson, Mark, and Ray Hosler. *Triathlon Training Book.* Mountain View, CA: Anderson World Books, 1983.

Nutrition/Exercise Physiology

Anderson, Bob. *Stretching.* Bolinas, CA: Shelter Publications, 1980.

Haas, Dr. Robert. *Eat to Win.* New York: Rawson Associates, 1983.

Kraus, Dr. Hans. *The Causes, Prevention and Treatment of Sports Injuries.* New York: Playboy Press, 1981.

Mangi, Richard, Peter Jokl, and William O. Dayton. *The Runner's Complete Medical Guide.* New York: Summit Books, 1979.

McArdle, William D., Frank I. Katch, and Victor L. Katch. *Exercise Physiology: Energy, Nutrition and Human Performance.* Philadelphia, PA: Lea & Febiger, 1981.

Morella, Joseph J., and Richard J. Turchetti. *Nutrition and the Athlete.* New York: Van Nostrand Reinhard, 1982.

Cycling Publications

Bicycle Sport, 3162 Kashiwa Street, Torrance, CA 90505

Bicycle U.S.A., P.O. Box 988, Baltimore, MD 21203

Bicycling, 33 East Minor Street, Emmaus, PA 18049

Bikereport, c/o Bikecentennial, P.O. Box 8308, Missoula, MT 59807

Cycling USA, c/o U.S. Cycling Federation, 1750 E. Boulder Street, Colorado Springs, CO 80909

Cyclist, 20916 Higgins Court, Torrance, CA 90501

Velo-News, Box 1257, Brattleboro, VT 05301

Winning: Bicycle Racing Illustrated, 1127 Hamilton Street, Allentown, PA 18102

Cycling Organizations

American Bicycling Association, P.O. Box 718, Chandler, AZ 85224

Bicycle Institute of America, 122 East 42nd Street, New York, NY 10017

Bicycle Federation, 1055 Thomas Jefferson Street N.W., Suite 316, Washington, DC 20007

Bicycle U.S.A./L.A.W., 10 East Read Street, Baltimore, MD 21202

Bikecentennial, P.O. Box 8308, Missoula, MT 59807

International Association of Triathlon Clubs (IATC), 301 East 79th Street, Suite 30-D, New York, NY 10021

Professional Racing Organization (PRO), 1524 Linden Street, Allentown, PA 18102

Triathlon Federation/U.S.A. (TRI-FED), P.O. Box 2461, Del-Mar, CA 92014

United States Cycling Federation (USCF), P.O. Box 669, Wall Street Station, New York, NY 10005

About the Author

Daniel Honig is president of America's leading triathlon club, the Big Apple Triathlon Club (New York), publisher of *The Tri-ing Times,* and founder of the International Association of Triathlon Clubs. He is also the author of *How to Run Better* and *How to Swim Better,* and is on the board of directors of the Triathlon Federation/U.S.A. He has completed ten marathons and thirty-two triathlons—ultra-endurance events involving swimming, cycling, and running in succession—and works with runners and triathletes of all levels. He is a pioneer in the triathlon movement, and his fitness lifestyle is an inspiration to many.

The author has been involved in athletics since his childhood. Through the years he has pursued the sports of cycling, swimming, running, tennis, cross-country and downhill skiing, kayaking, and sailing, and has earned a brown belt in karate (shotokan style).

He received a master's degree in Operations Research from New York University in 1971. Since 1972 he has worked as an international marketing director, lectured in industrial marketing, and started his own marketing consulting firm.

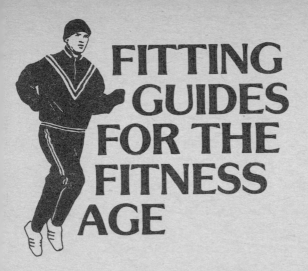

FITTING GUIDES FOR THE FITNESS AGE